Life Dances

ALVIN AILEY AMERICAN DANCE THEATER

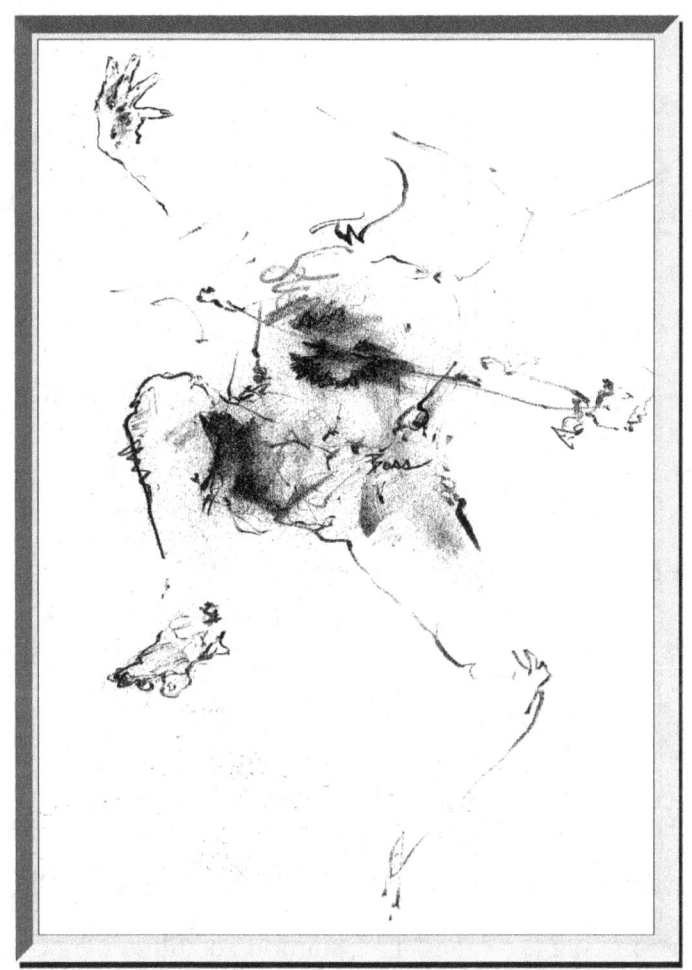

POETRY
REMEMBERING THE COMPANY'S SECOND DECADE

ROBÉRTU RAS RILEY

Celerus Books

© Copyright 2014, Robértu Ras Riley

All Rights Reserved.

No part of this book may be reproduced in any form or by any means, stored in a retrieval system, or be transmitted by any means, electronic or mechanical; this includes photocopying, recording, or otherwise, without written permission from the author.

For information, contact Celerus Books at
info@fidelipublishing.com

Celerus Books is an imprint of Fideli Publishing, Inc.
www.fidelipublishing.com

Cover drawing and drawing on page 161 by Lowell Quentin Bass
Artwork credit page xxxv, 27, 69, and 133, Ramon Akaulitzki via CanStockPhoto.com

ISBN-10: 1-60414-003-8
ISBN-13: 978-1-60414-003-3

Author's Note

Life Dances is a book of poetry which captures the world-famous Alvin Ailey American Dance Theatre from 1970-1980. The Introduction starts where the critics first begin to call Alvin Ailey a "genius," just after his company returns from its triumphant tour of Russia, "the first American modern dance company to go behind the Iron Curtain." The fact that this is a "black" company makes its success even more significant. Robértu Ras Riley was close to Alvin Ailey and his art. He was his friend, fellow artist, and a fan. In this section of the book, he describes Ailey and his choreography as he struggles and creates against the background of national and international events of the 1970s.

The poems are about the Ailey dancers, mainly; their lives, their classes, their rehearsals, their talent, and their magnificent performances. There are poems about dance teachers, patrons, benefactors, and famous choreographers from other dance companies commissioned by Ailey to create works in his own company. Everybody who was associated with "the great Alvin" has been included: Leonard Bernstein, Harry Belafonte, Jacqueline Kennedy Onassis, and others. There is even a poem about "Intermission." There are poems to "the times that we lived in as black people." In 1970's America, African-Americans still held on steadfastly to the hope they had derived from the 1960s. Alvin Ailey American Dance Theatre is where that hope lived, where it was taken into full account and made into art.

At the end of the book, there is a *Postlude* to one of the company's most famous dancers, Ulysses Dove. There is also a surprise *Encore!*

Table of Contents

The Introduction xv
    Ode To My Poem On Tour (With The Alvin Ailey American Dance Theater) xxviii

LIFE DANCES

The Women

Body Song	1
Saturday Night Dance	2
Waiting In The Wings	3
Sara La Divina	4
Sister Girl	5
Dance Fantasy Romance	6
Michelle	8
Star Dancer	9
Linda	10
Tina	11
Jodi	12
Nerissa	13
Ronni	14
Wa Boppa Lu Boppa Lam Bam Boom	15
Soul Dance	16
Bella Donna	17
Lady Sarita's Flamenco	19
Prima Donna	20
Night Creature	21
Good Rockin' Mama	22
Standard-Bearer	23
Madáme	24
For Consuelo	25
Ailey Girls	26

The Men

Ease In Motion	29
When Dudley Dances	30
Classic	31
Black Tie	32
"Blood"	33

Night of the Latin Quarter Moon	34
Enamorados (A Fantasy)	35
Guess Who I Saw Today Walking Down The Street In New York City	36
In Winter I'll Remember Summer	37
Good Buddy	38
Still Life	39
Kakemono in Motion	40
Oka	41
Soul Brother	42
Call Of The Kookaburra	43
Solo	44
Mel Movement	45
Blues Song	46
Poem For Alistair	47
Roman	48
Sundance	49
The Spin-Around-On-A-Dime Champeeen	50
Kenney Dance	51
Danny Dance	52
Milton Dance	53
Kevin Flow	54
Dance Of Joy	55
A Simple Elegance	56
Combination	57
Fire Dance	58
Body Painting	59
Elbert's Poem	60
Message Of The Rhythm	61
Life Dancer	62
Dance God	63
Poem Dances	64

Life Dances

Life Dances	71
The Impresario's Promise	77
Opening Night: The "Getting Ready" Overture	78
Dance Of The Seven Rhythms	85

The Night You Danced At The Gala	86
Intermission	87
Cry	88
Wade In The Water, Children	92
Mothercountry	93
Come Dance The Juba Looney	96
Commentator	99
Dance A La Eleo	100
"Sounds In Motion"	101
The Director-Choreographer At Work On A Musical Play	102
Ode To A Dancer	104
Stage Door Johnny	106
Donnie o'	107
Falco	108
Mama To The Dance	109
The Dance	110
The Conductor	111
Maestro	112
"Brother John"	113
Belafonte	114
Life Dances	116
It Was A Cold And Dark And Dreary Night	117
Valley Of The Shadow	118
Star Pupil	119
Movement	120
Pastorale	121
The Best Music You Ever Laid Your Ears On	122
Disco Ritual: Circa 1976	123
Antonio Et "Le Jardin"	125
Matinee Idol	126
Star Dance	127
Cake Walk	128
Joan Of Art	129
On The Road	130
Life Dancers	131
Forever Yours	132

Postlude

More Than "Just A Word Or Two" 135
Dedications 141
Dance All Around 150
In Order For The Dance To Continue 152
"A Time To Weep" 154
Everything Here Is Black And Gray 156
Instrument 158

Encore!

"RITUAL ONE: BLACKBONES BACKBONE" 163

Acknowledgments 172

Dedication

To Vera L. Embree
Who first introduced me to the world of dance

Who Better?
A FOREWORD

The good, solid, stylish writing of the poet gives *Life Dances* five stars. The book is about the Alvin Ailey American Dance Theater from 1970 to 1980. No pictures are needed to illustrate these poems. The poet is so gifted that he can make you see and feel his dancers even without photos. Robértu Ras Riley (formerly Robert Maurice Riley) was there. In a close and personal way. Who better to write (or speak) about the Company than Robértu?

It was Alvin Ailey himself and Ailey's friend, Harold Youngblood, who personally introduced Robértu to the New York dance scene in the 1970s. Youngblood was chairman of the Special Programs Division of the New York State Council on the Arts, which gave the Ailey Company most of its main support. Robértu accompanied Youngblood to weekly concerts of dance companies, big and small, and learned from everything he saw. Robértu demonstrated, applied, and taught the male dancers in the Ailey Company how to use make-up for the stage (his undergraduate degree is in Theatre and English). In return, Ailey gave Robértu complimentary tickets to whatever performances of the Company that he wished to attend. The dancers, both the young men and the young women, became close to Robértu. He wrote poems about them, as

Bwell as commentaries and reviews for magazines and newspapers. His impression of the Ailey Company today is as faithful and as elated as it was 30 years ago.

ack then, whenever the Company was "in town" (New York City), Youngblood would invite Alvin and Ellis Haizlip to dinner with him and Robértu at the "Coq au Vin" French restaurant on Eighth Avenue and 57th Street. Here, the four men would discuss dance, dance in New York, the Ailey Company, dance residences, professional dance schools-everything that was connected to the world of dance. Sometimes, they would be joined by Ed Lander, then the Executive Director of the Ailey Company, who came for more than just the socializing but mostly to hurry Alvin back to his rehearsal or because of some business that had to be finished right away. Haizlip, then the only black producer for Public Television, whose office was just around the corner, would bring everybody back to his office, and there they would enthusiastically begin writing into the evening yet another proposal for yet another grant for Alvin Ailey, who would now be happily and confidently back at his rehearsal. Years later, it was Robertu who helped convince Haizlip to invest $25,000 of his own money to commission the Ailey Company to create a ballet in memory of his (Haizlip's) mother and father.

Alvin Ailey personally picked Robértu to be among those who would speak during Intermission at many an evening performance at City Center in the mid-'70s. It was a time when the Company used Intermission to raise funds for itself. The speakers were called "Special Guests," and his or her job was to get, in the most creative fashion possible, audience members to leave a donation in the ushers' buckets on their way out. Robértu always closed his pitch with dynamic renditions of "black poetry." Some of it his own. Some not. In either case, it always got a rousing response from the audience. Ivy Clarke, Executive Director of the Ailey Company at the time, used to tell people that on the nights Robértu spoke, the buckets reached their fullest. Ivy had to approve the speakers and the speeches. Robértu was one of her favorites. In

Life Dances, he remembers her in a poem titled, "Forever Yours." It is one of the shortest but one of the most beautiful poems in the book.

The decade came to a forceful climax for Robértu, when in January, 1980, Judith Jamison danced his poetry at the Kennedy Center in Washington, D.C., with President and Mrs. Jimmy Carter and Jacqueline Kennedy Onassis in the audience. The dance was called "Inside," and was choreographed by Judith's fellow dancer-turned choreographer, Ulysses Dove. Critics said it was, "Jamison's greatest solo since 'Cry'." Since then, the American dance community has become familiar with Miss Jamison's great love of poetry. *Life Dances* is about one of the most fantastic times in American dance history where Judith Jamison was the center of it all. The Postlude in *Life Dances* pays tribute to the late Ulysses Dove and is dedicated to Miss Jamison.

— The Publishers

The Introduction

I want you to get deep and go back to the Seventies with me for a few minutes …It is 1970, and Alvin Ailey, 38, choreographer, and artistic director of his own dance company, and who has just stumbled out of the '60s (the decade of his greatest struggle), is about to begin the most prolific decade of his career. He is now, they say, "cooking." "On a roll." He is an artist whose mission it is, and was always, to create from life around him, or from his life's imagination, pieces that will cause all the beholders of his works to see that there are no differences between us, really, whatever our race or creed or color. He hopes that our understanding this will make us feel better about *"runnin' on,"* as the old Negro spiritual goes, *"to see what the end's go'n be like."* He can, especially, draw dances (pictures/images) from the deep-down beauty and greatness of his own African-American culture; and the beholders are able to see that this "Black Experience" is, actually, a reflection of the Human Experience. We urge everybody to "go and see Alvin Ailey!" We don't want anyone to miss out. His is a transforming beauty. Everybody agrees. Critics and audiences alike proclaim that, "Ailey is a genius."

Alvin simply smiles and takes it all in. His friend, Vera Embree, a former dancer with the early José Limón and Martha Graham companies, and now a professor of dance at the University of Michigan, continues to take it upon herself to open up more of the Midwest to Alvin and his company. But life in 1970 does not show Alvin any signs that things are going to get any better for "the people." Richard Nixon orders the invasion of Cambodia and splits us, the nation, in half. Students at Ohio's Kent State University riot about the war. The National Guardsmen come in, kill four of the students and wound nine more. Riots break out on campuses all across the country. Americans want peace. Alvin Ailey insists upon it. He has been listening to the music of Miloslav Kabelac. He takes his company into the studio and they work day and night until he is finished. He emerges with "Streams," a most peaceful, tranquil, and orderly ballet. The critics love it. "Ailey has created order out of the disorder in and around him and us," they say. But all Alvin talks about is how patient "the children" (his dancers) were with him as he worked. He dares life. When Joe Frazier wins the heavyweight championship from Jimmy Ellis, Alvin laughs and declares, "There you go! You gotta keep fightin'!"

As soon as he finishes another piece that he's been working, "Gympopedies" (Eric Satie music), the American Ballet Theater calls. They want Alvin "to choreograph a major ballet." He creates "The River" for them to the music of Duke Ellington and is, once again, hailed "a genius."

1971. Alvin continues to make art out of tragedy. The death of Janis Joplin becomes the inspiration for his "Flowers" ballet. Shadowy and psychedelic, it is a brilliant tribute to his favorite rock star.

In no time, he is making plans to embark upon "the midwestern tour." The company is still riding buses most of the time, and Alvin doesn't like it. He complains about committee meetings to go to; of still having to "outright beg" for financial support; and of having to continue to prove himself. He is a very busy artist, trying to be as responsible as he can. He finishes a piece called "Archipelago," and they leave.

When the company returns to New York, Alvin immediately goes into his studio and begins work on "Choral Dances." He, purposefully, finishes this dance on the same day that Congress gives 18-year-olds the right to vote. He is so full of work and creativity and production these days that he has not, for example, had a chance to buy a gift for his mother who is flying in for her son's company's spring opening. You probably already know the story. Alvin gathers up the music he's been carrying around in his head, grabs Judith Jamison by the hand, and, together, they head for the studio. For hours and hours, it is just the two of them, all the way. Finally, they come forth with a dance solo. Judith performs it on "Mother's Day" with Alvin sitting with his mother in the audience. He tells her that the dance is his gift to her. "It is called 'Cry,'" he says, "for all black women everywhere, especially our mothers." The dance is, also, "especially for" Judith Jamison. It establishes her as a star. We are overwhelmed by her intelligent and powerful portraits. As we leave the theater, we know that we shall never forget this "dance experience."

Some critics speak of Alvin "creating from his roots again." His response is, "Only partly." We know that he trusts and believes in the aristocracy of his ancestral legacy. "But our dances are about more than that," he says. "Our dances are about life. Yeah. *Life* dances. You may or may not find some elements of 'the Black tradition' in them." He and his "children" are "paintbrushes, instruments of beauty," he says. "I'd like to do a festival of dance to the music of Duke Ellington and show you what I mean."

Alvin is very open and true to himself and to his intentions. His art, therefore, is finely tuned to life. One day, three Russian cosmonauts are found dead after being returned from space in Soyuz II. The next day, Alvin's "Mary Lou's Mass" appears. "Imagine seeing a mass in the music of Mary Lou Williams," a critic writes. The bold, prayerful, simple, sturdy movement to a sound that you, somehow, just know is "black" *and* "American," passes before the eyes — and upon the ears — of a saddened world and lifts it.

Henry Kissinger flies to Peking and relations between the United States and the People's Republic of China, hostile toward each other for more than twenty years, get suddenly and dramatically better. And thousands of miles away, back in New York City, Alvin Ailey bows his "Myth" to the music of Igor Stravinsky. And when *The New York Times* publishes the Pentagon Papers, the Joffrey Ballet Company opens its new season with Alvin's "The Mingus Dances"; a tribute to the brilliant Charles Mingus. Normand Maxon, Alvin's closest friend "from the early days," asks Alvin at a Christmas party if he realizes that in this one year alone he has choreographed seven major dances, the most he has ever done in a single year. "Yes, I do realize it," Alvin says. "I wanted to outdo what I did ten years ago." (He created five ballets in 1961.) "Now that I've proved to everybody and myself that I am sharper than I've ever been, I'll probably never do it again."

1972. Life's terrible music continues to play. No sooner than West Germany releases 5,000 doves of peace to open the Munich Olympics, do eight Palestinian terrorists break into the Israeli team's quarters, and kill, first, two of the athletes, then nine others, before they, themselves, are killed. Alvin Ailey, like the spirit of the Olympics, is on a peace binge, too. Lately, he has been courting the music of Ralph Vaughn Williams. The premier date of his new ballet will soon be announced. Everybody has great expectations. Finally, on opening night, it is presented to us under the title, "The Lark Ascending." The ballet is wonderfully smooth. The critics agree that it is "Ailey at his best" "Lyrical!" "A romance!" Once again, Alvin balances the world with beauty.

Now comes "Mass" to the music of Leonard Bernstein for the opening of the Kennedy Center Opera House in Washington, D.C. The huge color photographs and story in *Time* magazine lovingly portray the dancers to the nation and help to render the company unforgettable. Dancer Kelvin Rotardier's face becomes as recognizable as sports star, O.J. Simpson's…Next, Alvin choreographs "Shaken Angels" for Dennis Wayne and Bonnie Mathis; and a piece entitled "Lord Byron" to the music of Virgil Thompson.

"A Song for You" is the title Alvin intends to give to his new dance, a solo for Dudley Williams, the longest standing member of the company. He has been with Alvin eight years now. Alvin calls Dudley "a poet, a body versifier." This piece is especially for him. "It will show Dudley's interpretatively unique way with movement as I see it." They are only part way through the dance when President Truman dies at his home in Kansas City at 88. Civil Rights leaders and black Americans in general remember the late president's advocacy and friendship. Alvin remembers being "a young teenager" when he was president. "It was a time of innocence. We had just moved to California from Texas." The two artists return to the studio and finish what they set out to make. Dudley fills our hearts with love on the night he dances the solo. The audience is standing. We are quite loud in our gratitude at being touched by the profound sincerity of his performance. (The "Nina Simone section" of the dance is particularly pure in its playful and rather sad and longing innocence of the past.) "Moving sculpture," the critics refer to Dudley. "It is my love of his artistry that inspired me to mount this piece on Monsieur Dudley," Alvin laughs! But he is serious. "Love Songs," as the dance is sometimes called, is a telling, narrative poem. It is clean and unadorned; highly technical but honest, and opens all the way out. The dance's creation and performance is, ultimately, an act of spiritual purity. Dance historians write it down as "timeless" "universal."

It is not with the greatest enthusiasm that Alvin returns to the American Ballet Theater. He doesn't use the phrase "drag myself over there" exactly, but that's how it appears. It isn't that he is not inspired or that he will not enjoy the experience. It's "Ellington" on his mind. And in his bones. He is back and forth on the telephone everyday about money and grants and proposals. And, although he can hire himself out these days for a good amount of money, it is not enough to compensate for being away from his company. Ivy Clarke, Alvin's executive director and general co-crusader, telephones Alvin with the news of the shooting of Governor

George Wallace in Laurel, Maryland. It is enough to prompt Alvin to make up his mind. Holding on to his music, he returns to ABT and creates "Sea Change" on the company. It is a ballet of much introspection, set to the music of Benjamin Britten.

Carmen DeLavallade, Alvin's premier dance partner and "sister," asks him one evening if he is going for another record. "No," he tells her. "Six is enough for this year…Besides, it is Christmas. Come shopping with me." He tells her that the Metropolitan Opera wants him to choreograph George Bizet's "Carmen" next year. They will pay his price. Ivy assures Alvin that the company's tour dates are solid enough for him to have enough time off to freelance. In the meantime, two giant pandas arrive at the National Zoo in Washington from China with love. Perhaps…

1973. No. Not yet. The President of the United States, Richard Nixon, is found guilty of involvement in a break-in of the Democratic National Headquarters in The Watergate building. Nixon's days in the White House are numbered…President Lyndon Johnson dies at 64 after a heart attack in Johnson City, Texas…Vice President Spiro Agnew resigns after pleading "no contest" to charges of income tax evasion. "What is going on inside people?" Alvin asks. "What are all these hidden rituals people go through?" When they ask George Burns, the famous comedian, what he thinks, he answers, "Too bad that all the people who know how to run the country are busy driving taxicabs and cutting hair."…Alvin puts his questions aside and choreographs "Carmen." Critics call the dancing "sensual, well-blended." Still, the questions. They have not gone away. And, still, he cannot answer them. First, he must make another dance for another opera, "Four Saints in Three Acts," to the music of Virgil Thompson.

Soon the company is "back from tour." Now, let's have at some answers. Alvin's search, to the music of Patrice Sciortino, is rapid and intense. The ballet, called "Hidden Rites," looks more like a formulation and presentation of questions than it does of answers and enlightenments. It is panned by the critics when it opens. "Hidden *Wrongs*," they call it. "Complex." "I submit that it is complex," Alvin replies, "but trust me; it has a core. Maybe it's not 'finished' yet…I'm going to get back to it." "Not soon," says Ivy Clarke. "CBS Television is ready to go with your dance celebration of Duke Ellington's music." "Fantastic!" exclaims Alvin. It is the beginning of a dream come true. The company works day and night. Word spreads down from New York to the national dance community that "the Ailey Company is before the cameras." Still, the critics' bombing of "Hidden Rites" remains to be quite a blow to Alvin. However, his following, his retinue, grows bigger.

By now, it is the last day of September. 1973. A plane lands at LaGuardia Airport from Detroit. The passengers unload. One of them is a poet, on his last leg. "What brings you to New York?" they ask. "Alvin Ailey," he replies. The influx begins…

1974. Richard Nixon, "with his lying self," is forced out of the White House; *and* the nation takes a good look at the Alvin Ailey American Dance Theater on television. God is good. The company never looked better. It is polished and finely dressed. The production "looks like somebody spent some money." The name "Alvin Ailey" becomes a household word…In the meantime, down in Atlanta, it is all Jesse Jackson can do to hold Rev. Ralph Abernathy in his seat about Richard Nixon. "He told us that he was going to take crime out of the streets! He did. He took it to the damn White House!" retorts the Rev. Abernathy.

Weeks later, Alvin is holding a news conference. The room is small. It is full of reporters — staffers and freelancers. Meg Gordean, Alvin's gracious and diplomatic publicist, has been as democratic in her selection of those-to-let-in as she can. Alvin is explaining his plans to adapt some of the television dances to the stage. The "Ailey Celebrates Ellington" festival will continue, he announces, on the stage in New York. "Yes. Judy will star," he tells the reporters. "*And* Sara…and, yes, Estelle. And I have asked another young and exciting dancer to join us, Sarita Allen…Yes, for the past couple of years, before he became ill, Duke and I talked about this project. It was a wonderful time for both of us. He was very excited over the idea of my making and staging dances to his music…Yes, Carl (Paris) will be in it. And Ulysses. And Peter. And Melvin. And Warren. And Alistair. And Clive, of course. All the children you love will be there to thrill you. Maybe Hector (Mercado) will even come back…" Alvin's charm fills the room as he happily answers one animated question after another. A reporter tells him that it has just come over the news that "Mikhail Baryshnikov, 'a dancer of great power and grace,' has just defected from the U.S.S.R." "See? See? Everybody wants to dance with the Ailey Company." The reporters are all tickled. "Seriously, though, New York is the dance capital of the world. This is the place to come and study and dance," Alvin concludes.

All those grown, black men, who were nearly-out-of-their-prime-to-start-with-but-left-their-good-jobs-in-other-cities-anyway to come, at last, to New-York and *dance* are, now, settled into "dance-related" jobs. Today, the younger ones arrive almost daily from across the nation. Some of them can hardly wait to be graduated from their schools or conservatories so that they can head for "The Big Apple" right away. "The hottest thing to be in New York today," Alvin says, "is a young, talented, black, male dancer." And they are everywhere. Black dance companies abound. They still struggle, but some manage to flourish. (Arthur Mitchell's Dance Theater of Harlem is beginning to enjoy its biggest success ever.) Alvin's company is the "big daddy" of them all, however; the *premier des troupe*…Hank Aaron breaks Babe Ruth's record with a 713th home run, retires from baseball and calls Alvin up to ask if he (Aaron) can be the spokesperson for his dance company! "They're coming from everywhere!" says Harold Youngblood, who is the director of the Special Programs division of the New York State Council on the Arts and mentor to many performing and creative artists.

1975. The groove is on. "Black" is surely beautiful. It runs all up and down Broadway, beginning with George Faison's beautiful dances of "The Wiz." Donna Summer dethrones Gloria Gaynor and becomes the new disco queen. We dance all night to her sizzling "Love to Love You, Baby." ("'Disco,' says Robert Vare, "is the noun, verb, and adjective of the 1970s.") Frankie Crocker rules the airwaves via WBLS. We listen to him and "classy lady" deejay, Lamar Renée, on our "boxes" as they play songs like "Love Won't Let Me Wait" by Major Harris. *The* hottest disco in town is *Le Jardin*; and the hottest tune in the dance line-up is "Fire!" by the Ohio Players. We are reminded that it is most often our rhythm-and-blues music that so many people in this world depend on to sustain themselves. And when Alvin Ailey American Dance Theater opens its Ellington dance festival at New York's 55th Street City Center Theater ("Broadway" for dance companies), all of our Black American culture seems to come together in one place.

Opening Night (or as Alvin always calls it, "The Gala") and Otis, the center's grand doorman, are in great form. He reminds one of one's uncle, maybe; the one who keeps a little half-pint tucked away somewhere for a quick little nip every now and then. Sometimes, when he gets high enough, Otis announces loudly, but as discreetly as he can, that he "don't drink from no bottle, buddy! I drinks from a *flaçón*." He, then, pulls out a small, engraved, silver flask that Fred Astaire gave to him when he danced at the Lambs Theater down on 44th Street back in 1936. Tonight, everybody is "madám" and "sir." The lobby is jam-packed. Folks! Folks everywhere. But, mostly, there is us. Black folks, of all ages and classes and vocations. We are, again, gathered closely together. We see, and feel, that it has not made any difference in us since we've been away from each other, living in the larger culture. Our link to music and dance reconnects us. This liaison is "our common kinship," as Vera Embree talks about it. Tonight, it surfaces in our hearts, and we take pride in what is ours. True love resides…You can see it in the way we greet each other. "What's hap'ning?" we ask. There are others here, too—all of whom can legitimately claim some kinship. But, tonight, as we Americans who are black look at each other—so many years after the struggle and so many years into it—we see that indomitable, triumphant spirit about us. It is the foundation that tells us to go ahead and build, and that whatever we are working on with love can take us, even, to the stars. It is that thing that got us through slavery that says "Rise!" Always, "Rise!" Other people who are here tonight care as much about our progress as well. We see it not only in their *donation to the cause*, but, also, in the love and admiration manifested in their behavior. That is why they are "family," too.

Someone spots Mrs. Coretta King "stranded in the ticket line" of the lobby. Otis has a fit! He summons a company official, and Mrs. King is ushered right in…A limousine pulls up. It is Mr. and Mrs. Jamison, Judith's parents, all the way in from Philadelphia… The entire cast of the Broadway show, "Grease," is off tonight in order to be here…Another limo arrives. It is Jacqueline Kennedy Onassis. Mrs. Onassis is dressed in black, floor-length taffeta. People's mouths drop at the sight of her. It is the very first time most of us have seen "our" First Lady in person. Immediately, images of the funeral of "Camelot," that time so many Thanksgivings ago, come back. Some of us, remembering her heroism, quietly start to chant, as we did back then, "Jack-ie…Jack-ie." She quietens us with a discreet wave of her hand and a smile. The man who is with her loves it. Otis takes complete charge…Lena Horne arrives. She is breathtakingly beautiful. As she passes, heads turn like cameras…Arthur Ashe and his beautiful wife, Jeanne, arrive…The striking couple behind them is Harry Belafonte and his beautiful wife, Julie…Nick Ashford and Valerie Simpson are mobbed at their limousine. It takes two policemen, and the help of Otis, to get them inside…Billy Dee Williams arrives alone. He looks great in his black tuxedo and red hose. Nobody can take their eyes off him…"Security" is finally called to clear the lobby. Nobody wants to miss an entrance…Ruth Ellington, Duke's glamorous sister, wearing diamonds and white chiffon, is splendid. She speaks briefly of her brother's greatness and his gratitude to Alvin. She thanks the various committees for their time and hard work on the project; and she assures us all that "Duke, still, loves you madly."

The company opens with "Night Creature." Later, it is followed by "The Mooche"; all to the luscious music of Duke Ellington. ("The Blues Ain't," "Sonnet for Caesar," and "Sacred Concert," seen on television, are not part of the stage celebration.) Flowers arrive on stage from everywhere and from everybody…Most of us know each of the dancers by name. As they go through their rushing, wavelike bows ("the *only* Alvin Ailey curtain call"), we become swept up, standing in the aisles, calling out their names as they concede their greatness. By the time the final curtain falls, we know that the world has said *"Okay"* to Alvin Ailey. He is at the top of his form. "At least, we don't have to ride around on buses anymore…Well, not much," he says, beaming.

Meanwhile, out in Sacramento, a secret service man manages to grab a young woman and pin her up against a wall before she can shoot President Ford…Three weeks later, a cop collars another woman in San Francisco after she misses Ford with her .33 revolver.

A few days later, a bomb blows up in the main terminal of LaGuardia Airport, kills 11 people and injures 75. What do we care about a little terror here and there! We got Alvin Ailey.

1976. The flower opens wider. The celebration continues. By the time Alvin finishes "Black, Brown and Beige," to music by Duke Ellington, we have elected a new president, Jimmy Carter. A huge black vote gives him all the South but Virginia. As we sit and watch the Ailey Company from our seats at the Metropolitan Opera House, the dances framed in a golden setting, we feel, somehow, that we are partly responsible for Alvin's success. And that's the way he likes it. "My success comes as a result of others' success before me," he states. "And just as their success was our success, my success is your success."

Some of the cannons you hear booming across the land to celebrate our country's bicentennial may well be the applause of audiences watching Judith Jamison and Mikhail Baryshnikov dance "Pas de Duke," a duet especially created by Alvin for the two stars who are avid fans of each other. Later, he will choreograph "Three Black Kings" to the music of Duke *and* Mercer Ellington, with sets by Normand Maxon and lighting design by Chenault

Spence. Alvin hasn't worked with his old friend, Normand, on anything since 1959… The three artists create a ballet that is a touching portrait of King Solomon, King Balthazar, and Martin Luther King.

1977. This is the year to tour and to do some personal travel spots as well. While Alvin is away, looters rampage, unopposed by the police, through hundreds of New York City streets during a 24-hour summer blackout. Alvin cables from Paris: "We're so hot now that we can't even leave the city without the lights going out. 'Turn up the lights. I don't want to go home in the dark,'" he says, quoting one of his favorite writers, O. Henry.

1978. And Alvin returns home from a Mexican vacation "and rest." He commissions the great American painter, Romare Bearden, to design the sets for "Passage," his new dance for Judith Jamison. Alvin is fascinated as he watches Romare work out his ideas. There are no more tickets left for Opening Night. Everybody wants to know if Alvin can still create for Judith. He can. She is magnificent!…After the spring season, Alvin leaves for Israel. There, he creates "Shigaon! Children of the Diasporo" for the Bat-Dor Company. Alvin and his Israeli dancers are proclaimed "heroes of the dance!"…He returns to his own company and takes on the biggest cast he has ever assembled. He uses his "first" company *and* his "second" company in a ballet entitled "Memoria." It is a sweeping, haunting tribute to his late friend and fellow dancer and choreographer, Joyce Trisler; set to the hugely elegant music of Keith Jarrett. Maxine Sherman's brilliant dancing and porcelain beauty keep her spotlighted as the dance's central figure. Her costume, a gown in white silk crepe, by Christina Giannini, is perfect. The critics go so far as to rank "Memoria" along with Alvin's "Blues Suite" and "Revelations," the company's signature pieces. "Memoria," like "Blues…" and "Revelations," also applies to the immediacy of life and death around us. The movement and its musical accompaniment seem to pay tribute now to the 914 people, most of them black, who died when a madman, a Rev. Jim Jones, talked them into killing themselves and their children by drinking "Flavor-ade," laced with poison, at his jungle settlement in Guyana. "Memoria" composes our souls. When a woman in England gives birth to the world's first test-tube baby, we know that life will go, tranquilly, on.

1979. Alvin is talking to me over the telephone. As usual, it is just after midnight. "Is this the poet-professor?" he asks, humorously. (He refers to me as his "poet-professor-actor-director-friend from Michigan." We met at the Detroit Institute of Arts in 1966 and have been friends—lunch, dinner, sometimes a party, but mostly by telephone—ever since.) "Alvin!" I say. "Whenever the phone rings at this hour, I should always know it's you. Where have you been?" He has just returned from London where he was a member of an international community of artists paying tribute to Great Britain's first woman prime minister, Margaret Thatcher. Alvin loves to discuss current events with me; and although I want to change the subject to dance, I don't. I know that he appreciates the opportunity to be "just a reg'lar guy." We talk about everything from the Pope's visit to New York to how Uganda dictator Idi Amin escaped when the local rebels and the Tanzanian army swooped down on him, "finally, after eight years," in Kampala. Always, before he hangs up, *Alvin* switches the subject to dance. He talks briefly about the company's past spring season, then he says, "...And now I think it is time for Ulysses to choreograph something for the company." (Ulysses Dove is one of the company dance stars—and Alvin's protégé—who is garnering a fine reputation for himself as a choreographer. "Ulysses has a new idea that he wants to explore," Alvin continues. "*And* he wants to talk to *you* about his project." "Me?" I ask. "You," Alvin replies. "I've got to go now. I have an early appointment with Stanley Plesent and the board. Ulysses should be getting in touch with you in a bit...'Bye." Alvin hangs up..."Me?" I, quietly, ask myself.

"I am choreographing a new solo for Judy [Jamison]. It is about love and what happens *inside* the mind of this person between love and love. It is a very serious subject, and I would like to use your poetry in the dance itself. Would you be interested?" Ulysses Dove is telling me this over a dinner that I invited him to when he telephoned a few days ago and asked what would be a good time for us to meet. "Of course, I am very much interested," I tell him. Actually, I am quite flattered by Ulysses. He joined the company the same year I moved to New York, 1973; and he was one of my favorite dancers from the beginning. I admire the discipline and "economy" that show in his dancing. There is a sense of "correctness" in his every phrase that says, "This is how it's done." The choreographic skill in his ballet for the "second" company, the Ailey Repertory Ensemble, is particularly outstanding. Ulysses is most knowledgeable in his conversations about dance with other dancers. They listen attentively to him. They know that he knows what he's talking about.

He is so naturally suited to what he does…"Then it's all set," he says. "You and I will schedule times to meet. We'll talk about love and certain specific emotions associated with love like 'hurt' and 'fear' and 'anger'; images I want the dance to convey. And later, when I leave, you can transpose these feelings into poems."

We are engaged in one session after another. We explore what 'hurt' feels like, what it does to the mind. Ulysses leaves. Two days later, I hand him a poem whose first line is *Spirit is the first target of hurt* … He loves it. We are on the right track. We go on for days. Talking and writing. Ulysses changes his mind about something. I listen carefully. I want to honestly hear him. We are artist-to-artist in this together. "A dance is being built around *my* poetry," I say to myself in the middle of the night. "Maybe," I think, "this will be the big one that will do it for me. After a couple of false starts Off-Broadway when I first got here, and another one just a couple of years ago, maybe this time … maybe … a dance for a star…" I fall asleep and dream. I see the children in Spanish Harlem welcoming the Pope. He is dressed in pure white with a long, regal red cape trimmed in gold stitching and flapping in the wind. "Bienvenidos, Papa Juan Pablo!" the children sing. The Pope stretches out his arms…

The next day, plans for me to watch the dance in rehearsal for the first time, and to listen to the music especially composed for it by Robert Ruggieri, are suddenly cancelled. I am disappointed but not upset. Days pass with no word from anybody. "What's hap'ning?" I ask the front office. Nobody is quite sure if anything at all is happening…Finally, I telephone my lawyer, the one that I have recently taken on after much persuasion and reassurance from him that he should be the person "to represent me as agent." I begin by asking how his meeting with the Ailey people went a few days ago. "When I walked in," he said, "I put the cards on the table, right off! I said to them, 'Gentlemen, let's be honest. What you're offering my client for this project is pebbles! We want more money.'"…Bill Hammond, now Executive Director of the company, explains that it is his understanding that "Mr. Riley has agreed to do this pretty much for nothing, for two reasons; one, it would surely be a step toward advancing his career, and two, this particular dance has a very limited budget." To which my lawyer replied, "Poppycock!" He continues with incident after incident in the discussion until someone calls him "totally disagreeable"…

"*I listen with heart fit to break*," as Browning says in his poem. Later, I hear that Ulysses was present at one of the meetings and had tried, unsuccessfully, to deal with my "difficult representative" and would have no more to do with him. It occurs to me now that Ulysses must have concluded that because of my representative he would have no more to do with *me* either. "Oh, well," I reason, "I have already given them what they need from me anyway." And after telling my lawyer how misinformed, inexperienced and peremptory I think he is, I fire him. "You know for a fact that I never wanted any more than a few hundred dollars for this," I add. "Your role was to simply see to it that my artistic rights would be protected. What you really wanted was more money for yourself. Goodbye" I say to him, and hang up the telephone.

I try to see the dance in rehearsal but I cannot. Other dancers in the company tell me that "the music is fabulous!" "It is a fifteen-minute workout for Miss Judy," one of them says. "And she hangs in there for the last drop of sweat." I hear that the poems have been "beautifully recorded" on tape by one of the two actors I recommended…Later, I hear that Alvin is back in town. I stop by his office, but it is not true. "Alvin is still in Paris," I am told. On my way out of the building, I hear that "the dance is finished"; that "it will go on tour with the company shortly after Christmas and open at the Kennedy Center in Washington, D.C., New Year's 1980; and that "President and Mrs. Carter will attend the opening night performance to welcome the star, the choreographer, the musician, *and* the costumer." No one, absolutely no one, has said anything about inviting me. I am truly hurt. Not even my anger can keep my heart from breaking…

Spirit is the first target of hurt (a line from one of the poems in the dance). On the day that the company leaves town, I walk, at times, aimlessly, through the streets of New York City talking Shakespeare to myself. "These words are razors to my wounded heart." It is still not my time, I think. "Will fortune never come with both hands full?" This project has been like the last match I have on me. When I strike it, it goes out just before I can use it.

I go home to my apartment up on West 94th Street. I go into the room where I write. It is cold. I think back to late summer when the Pittsburgh Pirates win the World Series in seven games with the Baltimore Orioles. It doesn't help. It is still cold. It is a long time before I can move…Finally, I pick up my pen and begin to write.

Ode To My Poem On Tour
(With The Alvin Ailey American Dance Theater)

I didn't even get a chance to see you
    finished
    before you left town
    complete
    like the man said he wanted you.
I don't even know who recorded you
    and put you on tape
    to speak to the people.
It's not that I was careless
    or anything dumb like that.
It's just that after they bought you
    away from me with their
    admiration baby talk and
    donation to the cause
They owned you
    and no longer had to be concerned
    about consideration and follow-up,
No longer had to acknowledge
    fingers that bore you to tender life.
And so I got word of you
    from here and there.
Someone saw you in rehearsal
    and said you looked good.
Somebody else said your costume designer
    was "ecstatic" over you,
"Couldn't wait"
    to get her hands on you.
Now I hear you'll make your first
    appearance before the world tonight
    in Washington, D.C.
The Kennedy Center for the Performing Arts
    will frame you like a portrait
And the President of the United States
    plans to put on a black tie
    to come and take a look at you.

Life Dances

Oh, look good, will you?
    But don't want it too much. Hold back
    to just this side of "amazing"
    and you'll be fine.
Keep that title, your head, up and smile.
    Bring out the hurt
    inside
    only when you dance and break their hearts.
Take your time and look around.
    This is your Big Moment (not mine, it seems).
Be cool and make even your faults look innocent.
    Remember, if they like you in Washington,
    they'll love you in Detroit.

Oh, how I wish I could see you.
    How I wish they had invited me.
    But sometimes people are mean.
They'll take only what they need,
    snub what you want to give
and hope the rest burns up.
    Realize that
Your going off
    (your having been *taken away* really)
    half-cocked is apt to perplex your reviewers,
    incite their disdain and ignite their hair,
Especially as you strut around
    on the subject of love.
    But stand up to them.
    You come from seasoned stock.
Say that they don't understand
    and keep on dancing.
    In the meantime, I'll stay
    inside
This cold room where you were born.
    I won't freeze. I'll take this paper,
    protection for my turned-out heart,
    and light another fire with my pen.

Movement, that problem of the visible arts,

can be truly realized by literature alone.

It is literature that shows us the body in its swiftness

and the soul in its unrest.

— Oscar Wilde

Life Dances

REMEMBERING THE ALVIN AILEY COMPANY'S SECOND DECADE

The Women

Ramon Akaulitzki

Body Song

Loose Not tight

Not pulled

And wound back   Or balled up

But loose   Clear   Like a carol

Like a breeze if you could hear it

Like a thrill if you could see it

Detached   Not snug

Not packed

And drawn up   Or trimmed

But flowing like summer's beauty

Unbounded   Gypsy bold

Like a spell if you could touch it

For Carmen DeLavallade

Saturday Night Dance

I never saw you dance
A flamenco
I never saw you dance
A waltz
Or a gavotte
Or a mazurka
Or a hora

Not even
A limbo at sundown
Or a reel
Or one of those dances that
Starts out flat on the floor
And turns into a big bright bird

But one Saturday night
Beneath the blinking summer thunder
I saw you dance a "backwater blues"
You did it with a belly roll strut

And I swear
I heard you call my name
And invite me inside your house
And tell me how wonderful I was
And couldn't I please stay for supper

For Hope Clarke

Waiting In The Wings

(...during Mr. Ailey's "Quintet")

It's like this

not like that

It's up here

not down there

It's two of these

not one

It's three of these

not two

It's over here

not over there

It's in

not out

It's getting *down*

not up

Ahn!

◯ *For Sylvia Waters* ◯

Sara La Divina

...after Mr. Ailey's "Lark Ascending"

Tonight, we see you as a lark
Ascending toward the temple of the gods.
The call has come down the sky
On the wings of a gold violin
And you have heard it.
You have taken the music out of the air
And held it to your ear
And made your arms wing-ready
For your high flight home.
We see the purple clouds of midnight
Drape themselves over your flex-flexing wings
As we watch your soaring song of joy begin…
0, you are mine alone!
A kiss in public,
A lost love found,
A courtship, a betrothal,
And in my wildest dreams,
A honeymoon.

For Sara Yarborough

Sister Girl

She takes her faith with her to hold court in the dance rooms she rules over,
careful to never overrule the hand that guides her through
the spirit of themes her body spells out in truth.

Her faith is her lucky piece that charms the eye
while she works her spell of deepness.

It is the rock that takes her back to the times when she watched the sun
disappear in the west behind nearly invisible horizons.

Times she spent paying dues,
before the goldpieces.

Times of her investment.

She takes her faith with her to the clear spaces she spreads
with her colour; spaces where she is lilting lovely lady in lilac,
a siren in red, or some slick-haired sexy Rexy's
pouting boogie woogie woman in black out for the hanky-panky,
hankering to live it up like real-life millionaires.

She will not remove the piece
she wears hidden under her gown.

It is her hold on the spirit of her ancestors
whose reputations she protects
each time she dances the faith.

For Estelle Spurlock

Dance Fantasy Romance

Was it in Rio that we met
And danced the *samba* in formal dress
Under a jeweled sky of sparkling jet,
Topaz and lapis lazuli?
It had to be there in my hotel room
Where I toasted you all night long
With cocktails from your black satin slipper.
And didn't we fill the Guanabara Bay
With cool champagne and bathe in it?
Townspeople exploded Roman candles
Above our heads,
"A toast to the young lovers!"

Or was it in Paris
Where I had been buying and selling
Diamonds one spring?
Was it there in the gold salons
Of Monsieur Guy de Doodeau that
I offered to trade you my heart
For your gem-glazed eyes
And you moved across the room
With the delicacy of a white
Feather in pearls and proper nylons?
Didn't you join me at my outdoor cafe
In the blossom-filled French air
In the afternoon?
And didn't we dance with the rest
Of Paris before you said goodbye?

Perhaps it was in Africa
That I first laid eyes on you.
My men carried you through
The junglebush on your safari
For photographs and fancy foreign intrigue.
I watched you dance the *unyagoni*
With village girls in native dress.
I taught you steps through my palace door
And, under candleglow,
You laughed in my arms.
Didn't we dance the *likembe mahoka*
To a thousand-year-old Swahili drum
Until dawn?

Or was it in Arizona
That we fell in love?
Was it under skies of technicolor
Blue and white and you in red
Buckskins running the Flying X Ranch
That I caught up with you once more?
I played your Randolph Scott
In the hot, cactus-filled backdrop
Of our global romance.
Weren't you the cowgirl who said
She couldn't be tied down?

Or was it in autumn in New York
One slick and drizzly night
At a Broadway opening?
And you were the girl in the limousine
And I was the guy on the curb
And I said *aren't you*
And you said *hello*

And I said *well bless*
And you said *still dancing*
And I said *yes yes*
And just as you leaned forward
Just as you reached up to take my hand
I woke up

☙ *For Maxine Sherman* ☙

Michelle

Yours was the dance
escaping in the night rain,
a clarion bell in a French tower
of some ancient cobblestone courtyard

Or it was one of those
sassy colored girl numbers
in red satin and purple mules
with hair worn like a crown

On a queen's head
aimed towards the future.

Echoes of you come back to us in visions
and my pen harnesses them,
gathers them up, ingredients for a poem
that say

We remember.

For Michelle Murray

Star Dancer

She wears a diadem
The color of gold sienna.
And lights, the color of jade,
Radiate from her eyes
Like a garden at noonday.
She is the polished star—
Shining
To brighten *us*;
To show *us*.

Tonight, under the staged moon,
She is a celestial body
Speaking to us in signs.
We follow her like no other.
She is a perfect example
And our eyes know it.
They waltz with her
Across the firmament…
And yesterday
And last month
And even an hour ago
Are all gone
On a star ride.

For Beth Shorter

Linda

I remember you especially
In "the house of the rising sun."
The light came straight through the window
And picked you out like a finger in an apparition.
Your long red brown hair suddenly moved
As though something had touched it
As if something had whispered to it
I am here.
It moved like your dance
And somewhere down the overall sweep of it
There was a wave, a dip,
A place where one could get caught
And tripped up if he didn't know
A quick-step from a one-step or a two.
…But *oh Miss Linda*

For Linda Kent

Tina

Caramel pink

set in art.

A softly played concerto.

A greenhouse

in winter.

Thoroughly bred,

beautiful, prancing

winner.

For Tina Yuan

Jodi

I saw your ribbons flow
In autumn of that year
Down the green and brown
Of a concerted stage
And dance about your fair
Maiden head as in a dream.
I saw you drift like a bird
Through the leaves
Scurrying under tiny funnels of air.
You moved toward me
Like a wind-filled willow.
Then, like a dancer in a cabaret,
You made me promise
To give you the world.

For Jodi Moccia

Nerissa

Not since uncle Lacy danced with niece Beora
Out under the chinaberry tree
On a starlit night one spring
And a mist covered El Dorado like gauze,
Coloring it blue, pale as heaven and as fleeting,
Has there been a sight dancing
As entrancing
As you.

For Nerissa Barnes

Ronni

An

Evening

As

Perfect as the month of May

As

Welcome as a woman in pink

As

Dramatic as a furious moon

As

Delightful as a new way of spelling

 For Ronni Favors

Wa Boppa Lu Boppa Lam Bam Boom

Left in the room
with nothing else to say
when suddenly the music changes.
She springs to the top of the
slick black grand piano dancing
as Little Richard screams
tutti frutti o rooti!
She is all the notes in his driving right hand
and all the ones on his funky left.
Play it like a man with the controls in hand,
she swings back to Richard,
and I'll dance it like a fire just breaking out.

For Shirley Black Brown

Soul Dance

It could have been Donna
    but it was not.
It could have been Linda
    but it was not.
It could have been Marilyn
    but it was not.
It could have been Sara
    but it was not.
It could have been Mari
    and it was, yes it was.

Her legs and feet were a locomotive
Moving in rhythm down the line,
Pumping its freight past the railroad sign.
Her spirit was the mountainside.
Her stomach was a rolling log.
Her torso, the place where the fire burned.
Her head was the engine.
Her arms were wheatfields.
Her fingers, blossoms in the wind.
And out of her mouth, words to the song:

"Everybody works outta dey own bag…"
Bobby Womack sings,
And her dance says,
"I can understand it, Bobby"
And Bobby sings,
"Somethin' cool but not too cold…"
And her dance says,
"I can understand it, Bobby"

Oh, it could have been Donna
    but it was not.
It could have been Linda
    but it was not.
It could have been Marilyn
    but it was not.
It could have been Sara
    but it was not.
It could have been Mari
    and it was, oh ladies and gentlemen,
    it was.

For Mari Kajiwara

Bella Donna

He had come to his seat in the theater
From a room in a sky-high hotel
Almost as tall as his too-tall dream
Cramped delicate overgrown dream
With edges that you can see from. Dream
Behind one window to the sky.
In his small room
Pretense runs into reality,
Sky-high hotel runs low
On spiritual nourishment
And escape becomes as essential as fresh air.

Tonight he has come to watch you dance.
His soul needs an intoxication,
A lifting and a livening.
Dance for him
And make him somebody.
Dance for me
And be my lady.

You came out of the wings
And poof the world was gone.
I stood in a garden
Made of moonlight and laurel
And shadowed by your ivy-covered window.
Harmonica love songs
And kisses thrown from under the
trembling tree.

Stardust on velvet cloaks
And a horse-drawn carriage.
White Spanish lace
And your promise on a blood-red rose.
I was Romeo
And *you* were my lady.

My pen, working undercover, painted you
Like some fine artist's brush:
High brown highbrow
Eyes like embers
Cheeks like a girl's
Mouth like a woman's
And a smile that said
Yes and no at the same time.
I was Leonardo da Vinci
And *you* were my lady.

I marched into ancient Rome
On carpets threaded with gold,
Unrolled before my feet by slaves.
I strode to the top of the senate steps
And spoke to the crowd on love and war.
When you appeared at my side
The people cheered, the queen! the queen!
I raised my arms and offered earth to heaven.
I was Caesar
And *you* were my lady.

I stood in the Hall of Justice
And wrung down the curtain on evil at last.
Changed Black and White into Only Right
And passed the Bill of Love.
I hailed you great among women
And changed your status to mine.
I was the President
And *you* were my lady.

"Chicken in the car and the car can't go
That's how you spell Chicago!"
Uncle came down from the Windy City
Every Thanksgiving Eve.
He drove a long blue Roadmaster
That could make you grieve.
Put on a smile, take off a frown.
Big Bo Riley was back in town.
Sweet, mellow woman by his side.
"I got nothin' to lose and nothin' to hide.
No thank you. Don't drink liquor.
It's too strong.
Smoke you some reefer. Lasts twice as long."
His suits were made to order.
Tweed by day, silk by night,
And "I love a fine, Christian gal
With all my might."
He danced the best jitterbug you ever saw.
"Nothin' in the rough,
And nothin' in the raw."
I was Uncle Bo
And *you* were my lady.

And after you had gone, and
After the people had stopped clapping, and
After all heads had been filled,
I left my seat in the theater
And returned to my hotel room sky high,
Somebody.

☙ *For Donna Wood* ❧

Lady Sarita's Flamenco

Sarita swirls, sways, curves her hips
Around and over the green wet garden
In her dress of lush orange ruffles.
She remembers the kiss, the lips of Hero
That glow like a dark red fire.
She remembers the honest eye of Hero
Caught in its polished conservatism
When he burns inside like a hot, raw edge,
Sharp enough to make his manhood a blade,
A cutting that comes through even in his smile.

Hero is the unrecognizable lover. And
Although he has ridden at the head of armies
In stiff black jackets and silver bells
At his shoulders,
He is unruffled by none of it.
Never bats his lashes or is baffled,
But is brave in front of his brigade
Charging to the banging of drums
And the clanging of irons.
But Hero can lay aside his armor
And take private charge of the bed
Where Sarita hides the fire
His passion rages to put out.
Hers is always the perfect fort
To check his savagery before he leaves
To reason with the world.

And when he steps into his high boots
And goes off to ride
The whinnying black horses,
Sarita sashays, stomps her pleasure
Into the ground,
Raises her arms in her ferocious dance
And thanks the wind of life
For her herald. Her hinge.
Her heart.
Her Hero.

For Sarita Allen

Prima Donna

She spills onto the floor
like a pail of confetti.
Tonight she is a star
and this is no act
(To *you*, maybe, but not to her).
Momma's in the audience
sitting next to Poppa.
Brother drove from Brooklyn
and Sweetheart is waiting in the wings.
Club members on the front row,
Ex-teachers on the second.
The rent has been paid for months in advance,
and the refrigerator is as full as a polar bear.
She got a raise yesterday
and top billing this evening.
And tonight, under this spotlight
that is hers alone,
she is going to renounce her inhibitions,
ball her shyness up like a wet paper bag,
toss her skirts to the wind,
and seize the stage like she's s'pose to.

For Marilyn Banks

Night Creature

They say the moon belongs to everyone.
Maybe that is true
For men who see clearly,
But for poets like me
You became the moon
That night you came down from the sky
And danced all over my senses
Pulling me around with you
Through the woods.
Creatures like you everywhere
Stealing hearts
And riding them up to the sky
On the wings of muted trumpets.
I reached for you
And a jive saxophone got in my way.
I called your name
And you danced off
With a lowdown clarinet
Around your waist…
You turned me on to moonlight and left,
Laughing like a bassoon,
Your friends behind you.
The best things in life are *not* free
In a fantasy.

For Sarita Allen

Good Rockin' Mama

She sparkles like pink sequins,
more suited for a tutu
than this sort of thing
sheer chiffon and a g-string,
but as every trouper knows
whether you dance in a ballet
or in a bar, you do the job
you were hired for.

The spotlight hits her hard
and won't let go. And it's do or
die. Openly. Out here in public
where the light only fades
when your act is over.

She picks up the rhythm with her fingers
to shake the dance out.
Her steps say
We're gonna aim for the light
on the ceiling.
First I'll give you a little twist
like this.
Then I'll turn
around
this way
and give you a little this
and a little this
and a big one o' these
and a big one o' these.

Then I'll drop down slow
down the middle
and do a little
grind.
Then I'll ease on back up
and float about a little bit
like this.
Then I'll pick up the time
on the piano
and shake over this way
a little bit. Yeah. Like this.
Now throw in a fast one o' these.
And two fast ones o' these.
Yeah. You got it.
You know what I'm talkin' about.
Good Rockin' Mama's got the joint jumpin'
And that light on the ceiling
is next.

For Sharrell Mesh

Standard-Bearer

We hear that the children
Must be able to do fifty spins
Before touching the ground,
Must be able to stop in mid-air
Until *you* say come down.
Must understand what Martin meant,
Must remember Malcolm's dent.
Technique *and* philosophy
Equal Aileyesque ability.
Mary Mary Extraordinary
How do your dancers glow?
With silver tights and colored lights
And a high-stepping chorus all ra'ring to go.

For Mary Barnett

Madáme

She regarded the floor where she made

Dances as a holy place.

It was the place where she gathered

Two and three and four and more in a circle

That held that bound that grew

Through the love thread she used

To weave a motion picture.

The floor was her canvas.

Its handsome grain

Needed no protection from her.

The floor was her temple.

It was the place where she came

To sanctify herself.

For Thelma Hill

For Consuelo

Remember

Remember

Remember

REMEMBER

Remember

Remember

Remember

Remember

Remember

Remember

Remember when she was the BEAUTY among us.

For Consuelo Atlas

Ailey Girls

Miss Donna
Miss Sarita
And Miss Mari.
Miss Marilyn
And Miss Sharrell, baby.
And Miss Maxine, honey.
And Miss Patricia.
Miss April, baby.
And Miss Renee.
Miss Danita and Miss Neisha,
Miss Deborah *with* an h
And Miss Debora *without* an h.
Miss Barbara P. and Miss Barbara K., baby.
Ailey Girls, sweetie.

And for all the others who ever were

Ease In Motion

Whether he was

A bolt of silk unfolding

Or a cascade of water,

A southern wind blowing northward

Or sparks falling on a holiday,

His dancing always put you on

The receiving end

Of a big hug.

For Jimmy Truitt

When Dudley Dances

He is a marketplace
Of color
One of those big flowers
In a Herb Alpert tune
That jumps
And kicks
And turns
And turns
And turns into
A twist
And straightens into
A walk
And leans back into
A slow old-fashion-
Cadillac-convertible-top type
Drop
And rolls into
A kick (you feel it)
And a jump (you fly up with him).
And life,
Blue black red used old and new life,
Dances before us like a painter at work.

For Dudley Williams

Classic

He would have been a velvet-coated
Boy in the Court of King James
Had he lived during the time when
Boys who looked like him were
Live pieces of sculpture that decorated

The thrones of the great and the famous.
Surely he would have been chosen
To sit near the head of state
Because he looked as good as he moved:
Grace
Handsomely drawn upon a bronze
Vase.
He would have even posed for Michelangelo
Had he lived in the fifteenth century
When beauty like his was admired
And celebrated in public places.

The artist would have thrown himself
At his feet to be the first
To capture this male rhapsody in marble.
Leoncavallo wrote of him as
Handsome harlequin playing in bowing grace

To saucy Columbine in nineteenth
Century, amber afternoons.
Leonardo da Vinci died with regret
On his lips because he never got
To paint him and leave his face

Next to the "Mona Lisa" he left the world.
Oh, how he would have danced
For David and his harp!
Mister Shakespeare would have written
   one more sonnet,
And good brother Beethoven
   would surely have finished
His symphony.

For Kelvin Rotardier

Black Tie

We knew that it could have only been
A cavalier like you who was permission'd
To dance with the fabled *Marielena*.

Only a man with soft grace like yours
Would be allowed to glide
Sensational beauty across shining floors

Of wood, under crystal chandeliers,
In polite society.
Only a man who dances with delicate charm

Like yours could even hold the hand
Of pureblood, harnessed maidens
In lowlight drawing rooms.

Your music is a grand piano
Tinkling pianissimo, hovering quietly
Underneath a brilliant bevy of violins

Labeled *Ladies* and *Gentlemen*.
Only a man who dances as deftly as you
Could smile and float

Through a jeweled dream waltz.
You are exclusive. Looks *and* line.
Bred from the best,

You are at home on anybody's stage,
Outdoor mall, concert hall,
Or palace ball.

For Clive Thompson

"Blood"

You a jazz solo
A hurtin' saxophone
A burnt chocolate melody
A liquid song
Composed out of the goodness
Of your soul.
You "the joint,"
The magazine under milady's bed
The real thing in a man's fantasy.
You Erotica.
You four hundred years of struggle,
Emerging.
You a baldheaded brother
Talkin' shit on Lenox Avenue.
You a big black ass
You a bass guitar
You bad.
You the "Negro National Anthem"
You the music "After Hours"
You a gray misty dawn over Manhattan
Billowing out of a distant mountaintop
And ascending into the orange of morning.
You the last time we heard a rooster crow.
You a fresh warm poundcake
And southern fried chicken.
You a merchant of good will,
The first version of everything.
They call you "Original"
But we call you "Natural."

For John Parks

Night of the Latin Quarter Moon

The night of the Latin quarter moon
Posed with love over the top corner
Of Manhattan in mid-October, early-
Morning frost, tinged with big-city
Poisons, but harmless to our nostrils,
Coated with the spray from warm lemon
Wines and smoke from the bosoms of hot,
Wild fires, fires, fires.
Isabella, Carmina and Hector hold the
Corner of Spanish Harlem in their rhy
Thmic hips that bob to drums that burn
In their bones like bongos. Isabella
Stands like a queen among the ruin,
And Carmina says, *I want to go home.*
This moon hanging in mid-October mad
Ness is too much for Carmina,
Daughter of the deposed Guido
And sweetheart of Hector, hero to
Caramel honeys that scream and melt
From his damp, redeeming touch. Now,
He cools the passion in his blood by
Keeping step to the sounds. His eyes
Flash across the Latin night like
Lights in an autumn disco.
I want to go home, cries Carmina.
Look at the moon, orders Isabella.
And Hector dances.

 For Hector Mercado

Enamorados (*A Fantasy*)

I have walked with you along
    all the cobbled streets of Madrid
    in Castile nights.
I have watched you in the afternoon
    lead the Paseo
    into an oak and silver arena
    to fight the bulls.
It was you who replaced all the leading men
    in all the "Blood and Sand" movies I saw.
Neither Tyrone Power or Robert Stack
    could have ever played their roles
    as well as you.
When night fell again,
I met you in the center of the public square—
    deserted and rainswept with olive leaves.
I was Intrigue, himself, in a trenchcoat,
    foreign and beret-headed.
I brought you a gold chain
    for the bulls you killed.
    "Wear it at your throat."
Like your name, you braved a smile.
    I took your arm, and,
Like the night, caught fall's fresh breezes
    in our dampened faces.
We wandered past the empty corrida
    and lingered.
I lifted your famous body over the benches
    in the grandstand, and
I heard them playing a song,
    "*Para dos espiritus bello*,"
On magical, strumming guitars.
    The time was right
Under sparkling, blueblack Spanish stars; and,
Like the stars, we lit up.

We visited Ava Gardner
    at her villa in the hills;
    drank the autumn wine
    and fired the early Spanish morn
    with toasts;
    then said "goodnight"
And raced each other home
    before the day broke,
Remember?

We left Spain in the winter
    and sailed to Enseñada,
    following the sun.
I chartered our course on the Spanish Main
    along the north coast of South America.
We supped on peppered beef and pimiento
    in Puerto Rico, hosted by the house
    of your grand family.
Hot wine in your veins, you spun a dance
    of lightning
    before our eyes
    before we slept.
We set out again on the Caribbean sea,
    two smiling sultans, tanned
    and drifting into Guadalajara,
    running barefoot through Tetuan.

Remember when we braved the sun with love
Platonic?
I promise to show you Marrakesh
    after next season's end,
    after the bulls have stopped baying…
I promise.

For Hector Mercado

Guess Who I Saw Today Walking Down The Street In New York City

I saw that boy from D.C.
Spring in his feet
Love in his heart
Talent in his legs
Dance on his mind
Dream on his back

Looking to be opened up
And realized.
Boy walking down the street
On his way to
"Mister Ailey's dance class"
Confidence in his head
And a dream on his back.

For Charles Adams

In Winter I'll Remember Summer

In winter
I'll remember summer
When the hour was hot
And I met you walking up Broadway.
I'll remember your pure call of my name
Coming straight from the heart,
Unaffected by any mental process.
I'll remember the touch of your hands,
Wholesome as bread.
And your smile,
Fresh as a new piano.
The summer breeze, soft as dawn's breath,
Christened our fellowship,
And then we said "so long"
Like a dance that ends…

In winter
I'll remember summer.
I'll light my midnight roof in candles
And build a purple fire
Bright as Venus
Above the red veneer of New York City.
And there in the royal gray wind
Blanketed under a magenta sky
Studded with stars of rhinestone and ice,
By the light of a moon
As big as an amber balloon,
I'll remember summer
And dance with you all the winter-night long.

For Keith McDaniel

Good Buddy

That summer
I saw him walking under the sun,
Eyes full of sunny weather,
Handsome in his bronze beauty,
Gleaming like a medal.
I saw him
Grin through his clean heart
And place his perfect hand
On my shoulder.
"Here is light," he said.
And there was.
"You are safe here."
And I was.

For Melvin Jones

Still Life

Cristobal:
in repose
slender leather strap
whiplash of energy
formerly of other floors
under other lights
in other houses
now of these

pauses and perspires
ivory colored beads

Cristobal:
waiting his turn
face explaining its body
glimpses of a mind packaged
in carmine and gold

reclining caballero
with stains of dirt
and flower petals
smeared across his
caramel colored and
chiseled hands

For Christopher Apónte

Kakemono in Motion

You are the sound of thunder
Quiet in the distance.
We have seen your leaps
Flash across the sky
In moving pictures
Like a prince in his
Father's boots.
Your mark is as precise
As swordplay.
We are pleased to watch you
Show off the silver skills
The royal flow
The gentle nurturing
In The Grand Manner of your
Western garden, second only
To your Eden of the East.

Kä ke mó no: an exquisite Japanese hanging inscribed with pictures

For Masazumi Chaya

Oka

The West
    bathes in topaz
    from starlight out of
The East.
    Oka dances
    and we watch him
    in a theater
Somewhere
    clapping our hands
    and smiling
    as every few seconds
The light
    of the
    star
    flashes.

For Michihiko Oka

Soul Brother

Oh, You
blend with Me
harmoniously,
like landandwater.
Different textures
but each
a part of the other
making a whole.
An intimate mingle.
A natural mosaic.
Beauty
of the figure
can have different lines
but
beauty
of the soul
fades the lines of difference.

For Michihiko Oka

Call Of The Kookaburra

I fashioned you in another time
A man who used to steal away into the woods
Of a winter night. There
You would pretend to be The King of Dances.
The kookaburra would watch as you strutted about
To the sound of grand coronets
In a cardinal coat of fur,
Majestic as your own appearance.
You moved within your stories
Of great woodsmen and hunters of the North forests
As Man in harmony with Nature
Not Man against…
You bowed in summer splendor to people
Who came to see your natural works of art,
But the kookaburra knew your story
And laughed loud.
Your hands looked too expensive to open and close
In extremes of heat or cold.
Your fingers and toes were meant
To snap and tap in dance
Yet to come in another world:

This one
Where you have brought your natural grandeur
Of polo coat living to modern dances.
The smell of pine and partridge berries is gone.
Your eyes into the future
Are as clear as winter spearmint.
And the call of the kookaburra
Is only an echo now.

For Peter Woodin

Solo

He always makes sure his music
Never gets too far away from him.
He even carries it around
In his fingers to spread a place
To dance upon.
Sometime he hitches it high
Above his head and
Dares anyone to take it loose
Before the lights go down.

Tonight
You can see the music rise
From the cup of his hand
And race up through his body.
It settles around an indigo arch of him,
A picture beginning to move.

He points his finger
To perfect music, pitched and cued,
And steps into the arms
Of his smiling god.

The room turns to gold
And we behold
A blue delight.

For Warren Spears

Mel Movement

Come and dance with Mel
He'll take you through a fast Merengue.
Look at his hips go.
Look at his knees, those precious links.
Look at the muscles in his thighs, working like tools.
See how precisely his sure feet slide.

His pelvis is a pendulum.
His shoulders are axles.
His arms are bars, protection from the fallout
Of oppression.

Come, he says,
Back to the place
Where the sidewalks are shaped
By the rhythm of our steps,
Where our feet have danced
To pain *and* to joy,

Where we have strutted
And fallen and
Risen
And kept on going.
Home,
Where, sometimes, our only food is dance.
Oh, Mel! Mel!

For Mel Tomlinson

Blues Song

Like a voice
And a piano
In an empty theater
He dances
Like a song
To the love
He misses
To the times
Out of lights
Out of costume
In feet free
From steps and
Positions

To the off days
The long nights
The loose time
With love

He dances.
His body is his voice.
Usually it rolls around
In the high notes
But this morning
In this cold rehearsal hall
It warbles the blues.

For Gary DeLoatch

Poem For Alistair

African loomed hair
On a proud head.
Face bright as a starstone.
Torso tight, long,
Limber as sugarcane.
Arms and hands like wings
On an island wind.
Rump smooth as boxing gloves.
Legs fast as a taxi.
Feet solid as marble,
And heart. *All* heart.

For Alistair Butler

Roman

Prince in white gloves.
Coat of manners.
Noble blood brother.
Bearer of fruit.
Squire with a head for harmony
And matching sketchbook face.
Sometimes a gentleman in ballet shoes
And always a star for good behavior.

For Roman Brooks

Sundance

"Oh Danny boy"
like the song

but like the universe,
too. Surely
like the sun.

Tonight
it reappears in the form
of brown charm

and beams us
all over. We bask in
your clear light

under a spell
that relieves
and lifts us up.

For Danny Strayhorn

The Spin-Around-On-A-Dime Champeeen

Step right this way
Ladies and gentlemen,
You of the hidden pain
You of the late hour
You of the first in line
You of the regained hope,
Turn your dark red hearts
In this direction
For the fastest action
In town.
See the man the world
Calls a wonder. See him
Dance like a player piano
Like a drumstick on a cymbal
Like rain off a roof.
This marvel
Who left them holding their breath in Europe.
This curiosity
Who left them rioting in South America.
This monster
Who killed them in Asia.
Ladies and gentlemen,
The hottest wind ever to come out of Cleveland
The one
The only
The legendary
Spin-Around-On-A-Dime *Champeeen!*

For Ronald Brown

Kenney Dance

When heads first turned toward Aquarius
And hair looked like grated coconut,
When spirits showed up in real life,
There he was—

A body as beautiful as a ballad,
With twinkly toes
And arms as long as a balance bar,
Ready to step and sway to music

Rich and thick as a succulent gravy.
His dancing always makes you think
That the sun has just come up,
And there you are—

Sitting, as alive as a cabbage;
And happy, for once,
To be exposed so directly
By such a loving brilliance.

For Kenneth Pearl

Danny Dance

More like a spiritual
than a blues.
More like joy
than pain.
More like testifying
than confessing.
More like melodrama
than tragedy.
Like Langston with a poem.
Or Aretha with her voice
around a song.
More like that.

For Daniel Clark

Milton Dance

Apparent

Sure-footed

Wingéd

Moving

Limber

Live wire!

For Milton Meyers

Kevin Flow

The sun just after
it has set.
Morning the second after
it has broken.
Earth after
a rain.
Eyes
dried.
The last note
of a song.
A painting
beheld.

∽ *For Kevin Brown* ∾

Dance Of Joy

His dance is touched with truth.
His body is a sacrifice of thanksgiving.
His high steps shout like a preacher
To the heavens
And arms of cheer dump the moonlight
Into our laps.
Revelry seizes him like a mother.
Triumph crowns his head.
Tonight his soul flings up its cap
And remembers joy.
Hail and hallelujah, we are glad!

For Ralph Glenmore

A Simple Elegance

He moves and he is a song
In perfect three-part harmony.
A cat's motion giving rise to

Images of a simple elegance:
A photograph in a pearl and gold frame
White linen and a monogram

A muted trumpet
Dawn in the country
Polished reality.

For Nat Orr

Combination

Steps
Like a jazz riff
Like something hot and risen
And waiting to be eaten.

Steps
Like a swirling hoop
Or a handclasp:

Classic moves
In modern time.

For Gregory Stewart

Fire Dance

Slowly,
Like a coil in a bedspring,
He curves around and leans
Upon the soft wool carpet
Spun underneath his belly
Like an orange cloud.
He slithers and gazes inward at himself,
Feeling the fuel in his veins ignite his bones.
His eyes glisten, flash
In the dark like fireflies.
He stands,
Posing like the statue
Of a man on a horse,
And mounts his invisible steed,
"Spirit, Lord of the Sky."
His legs, big as columns, absorb the rhythm
And rush it to his brain.
There a fire starts that only dancing
Can extinguish.

For Marvin Tunney

Body Painting

Presence and Skill

Combine to create

The picture before us.

All the colors

Move at once and be-

Come magnifical.

But our "eye"

Goes straight to you

As eyes are apt to do

When they spot

An original.

For Carl Bailey

Elbert's Poem

Your body is the animated speaker
For the music.
The music plays
But it is not to be listened to.
Tonight, it is to be seen.
You move. Your dance is a poem.
It reads across the footlights,
All the way up to the last balcony.
Oh, we can hardly wait to take the good news
Back to the children!

For Elbert Watson

Message Of The Rhythm

Who's this with the wiggles?
Who's this with the shakes?
Who's this whose arms turn like wheels?
Who's this whose pelvis pumps like a motor?
Who's this who's trying to be so cool?

Not you.
Not Don Juan in the velvet britches.
Not The Slow Dance Kid.
Not The Song of Songs.
Not *Monsieur*.

Well, it looks like you go, too.
This ol' rhythm don't discriminate.
It likes blue eyes big lips sharp noses and brown skin,
Black hair blonde hair slanted eyes flat feet
And cool, *not dead*, heads.
Its clear message is

Life dances!

For Ronald Dunham

Life Dancer

Dues
For services rendered
And unrendered.

Here go de rent
Here go de lights
Here go de telephone
Here go de food
Here go de clothes
Here go de remedies
Here go de upkeep
and another pound of flesh.
This morning I dance and my body
must tremble like a flute.

Here go de neighbors
Here go de acquaintances
Here go de well-wishers
Here go de friends
Here go de tutelary saints
Here go de bosom buddy
and another pound of flesh.
This afternoon I dance and my body
must bend like a reed.

Here go Mama
Here go Daddy
Here go Angel Number Four
Here go love
and another pound of flesh.
This evening I dance and my body
must warble like a bird.

Here go de boss
Here go de assistant boss
Here go de performance
Here go de job
and another pound of flesh.
This night I dance and my body
must work like a machine.

Here go de body.

For Melvin Jones

Dance God

And somewhere

in the crying jet night

he was the red meteor

we saw dancing

with a starlit umbrella

under the pouring yellow dust

of a strobe-lighted moon

and a night-white cloud—

high, high up

in the blackblue sky

where he had flown off

to dance for the peace

of men of women

of worlds to come.

☙ *For Dudley Williams* ☙

Poem Dances

My poems are movements

Making their way through

Choreographed settings,

With plots rising

On moving climaxes,

Searching through conflict

To make some human point

Like an Ailey dance

That begins

And ultimately resolves

And ultimately defines.

"Happy Birthday, Judy!"

20th Anniversary

May 10, 1978

Photo by Susan Cook

Alvin Ailey surprises his young star, Judith Jamison, with flowers and hugs on her birthday on stage at New York's City Center. Gathered around them are company members (l. to r.) Clive Thompson, Mel Tomlinson, Marilyn Banks, Jodi Moccia, Sarita Allen, Maxine Sherman, Nicky Harrison, Enid Britten, Dudley Williams, Melvin Jones, Dwayne Talley, Michihiko Oka, Beth Shorter, Ronni Favors, Milton Myers, Mary Barnett, Keith McDaniel, Donna Wood, Alicia Adams, Peter Woodin, Steve Moñes & Charles Adams. **The program that evening was "Streams," "Icarus," "Passage" (a solo especially choreographed for Judy), and "Revelations."**

LIFE DANCES!

Alvin Ailey rehearsing "Night Creature," Alvin Ailey American Dance Center, East 59th Street Studios, Manhattan, 1976

Photo by Susan Cook

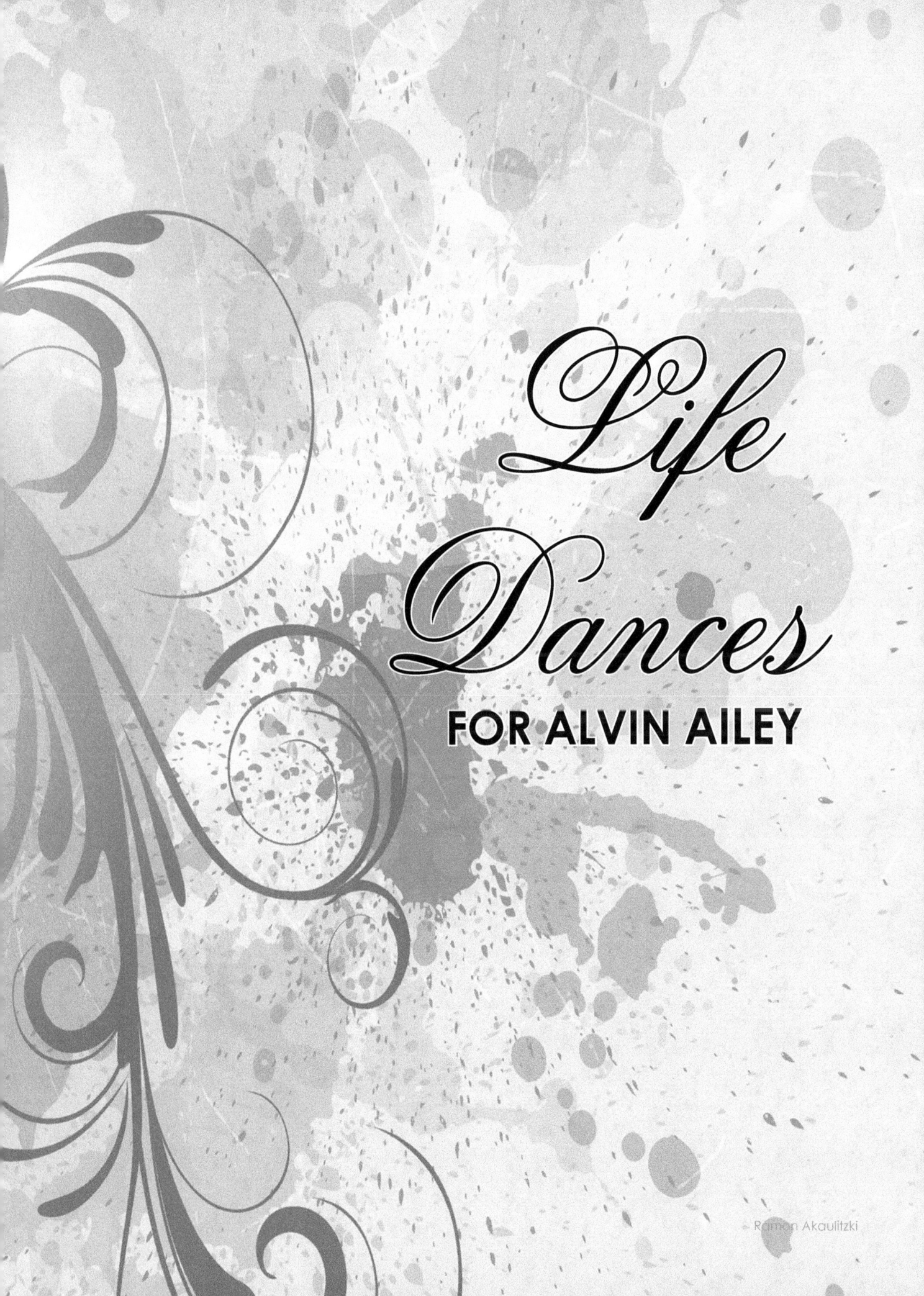

Life Dances

Steps fall under the movement
Like finding the parts to a puzzle.
The thought of what to do with them swirls slowly
Across the back of his brain like cake dough
In the slow low beat of an electric mixer.
The chocolate cream rich mix of his heritage and
Influences stands firmly on the tip of his tongue
And dances are born from out of his head:
The sinewy motion of musclemen
That he saw as a child;
Teasing Texas tawdries
With whom he talked in his teen years;
The honed and honeysuckle heart of Horton,
A heady art Alvin Ailey adds to life like Alladin.
The Style carries us to the mountaintop
Where we celebrate the Joy and Love of humankind.
We put on ancestral robes and blow our trumpets
As we find ourselves in every lively moment.
Our Selves are celebrated through his genius,
And his genius allows us to celebrate.

The dancers absorb the picture from him
And set the movement in heart, body and bone.
His magic takes me back to Worlds Known
And Might Have Been; Unknown,
Red floorboards I dare to tread with him;
Too Cold Too Hot Places asleep in foggy memory;
Worlds Behind Me and Worlds to Come
And all in Between is Magic, Light *and* Dark.

The fog clears the gold box that sits
High upon the curved reaches of my memory.
And I hear the music of Jump-South Jazz
And I see "Berry Black Annie,"
Arkansas Shakedancer,
Bringing "her best of Broadway"
To wooden rooms of chicken shacks.

Clearly "Miss Blackberry,"
Whose mystery satin skin promised
Sweet secrets,
Whose tiny jet eyes promised
Raw discoveries,
Whose head, despite the brief glitter it brought,
Had to hustle the rent she paid to live
Above the Days of the "Fifty-Two-Twenty Club."

To the times when the principal
Of Booker T. Washington High
Became the first Black man to speak
At the Kiwanis Club, and the high school
Dance group rendered their best, an African ritual,
And the newspaper called them "militants."
But the choir sang, "This is my country…"
And everybody smiled.

To Early Morning Service Easter Sunday;
To Christmas Pageants at First Baptist Church
When Bobbie Jean Jackson sang
From Handel's "Messiah" with class,
And Miss Laura Johnson was selected to dance

The Part of Jesus
Because her hair was longer than anybody else's.
To the music of big flowered, lace handkerchiefs
In the stiff white talcumed
Usher uniforms of "Mother Hattie"
Whose hands were filled with Welcome,
Whose heart was filled with Love.

To the times when Aunt Eliza Creer
Grappled with the Holy Ghost
And the spirit threw her dancing
Off the edges of the baptizing stream.
To the times of "The First Sunday in August"
When folks down home in country church spread
Dinner On The Ground to welcome us back
Who once escaped to the North and was
"Doing pretty good";
And "Co'n Myrtle" and Co'n Amma Lee,"
Cousins big and buxomy,
Wore yellow and white dresses of voile
And wiped sweat;
And "Aunt Sarah," grandmother to me, and
Widow of the late "Uncle Lacy," came
All the way down from El Dorado and was
"Doing pretty good";
And "Mama Sallie," Midwife to All
In present flock, holding me on her knee,
Blessed her children, and said,
"Stay out of bad company, and
Don't do nobody wrong," said,
"Remember the Lord loves a song."

And Jesse and Clara Hogan sang, "I *love* the Lord,
He heard my cry and pitied every groan…"
And the shepherd called his flock around
And preached the Word of Wonder
On How We Got Over Back Yonder
'Til the Spirit came. It burned the hearts
Of Uncle Donnie and Aunt Nellie
And they couldn't do nothing with Aunt Rye-Ethel
Who went outside behind the church-house
And danced until the Holy Ghost left *her* alone.

To the times when Miss Eula Vee,
Because she was a school teacher,
Called the police to keep the white folks
From holding their picnic dance
On top of her new rosebushes;
To Miss Eula Vee,
Who used to say to the world of me,
"This little boy can sure write prettily."
To the times of a Boy Poet
Who sat and watched quietly and deeply
The roots of a growing Blackness.

To the heavy springs when it used to rain
And Black people could not go dancing
Because of the mud. And if you had a car,
You were stuck for sure.
To Fast Alvonyun
Who dropped Swinging Gurtha Lee in the slush
On the night of the fancy senior prom.

To the times when I led the band on Halloween
And Miss Beulah Broadnax put on a false face
And danced like an Indian all night long.
The next day she told everybody that her
"Grandmother was a full-blooded Indian
And proud of it!"

To the place where Sweet Mavis sang
The evening the blueberry bushes burned.
To her dancing Wafer Tee
Who never made it out of the Fifties.
To lost and dusty Valentines…

The brasses on which I blow
Bespeak of triumphant souls I know:
Suntanned sons of Arkansas;
Daughters of kitchens and cottonfields;
River-rat dudes on Calion Lake;
Black, vested, pocket-watch paupers defying poverty;
Men and Women of Victories.
To the times when first we knew
That all our honors from the world
Of Book Learning
Had not buried our Heritage
To cry
To sing
To dream
To dance.

To dreams of my silver house in the sky
That sits in the clear and lofty blue
Where white clouds hover at the windows
And a golden chariot waits to take me dancing
Across the universe
To rule the World with Laughter.
Birth is a station.
Luck is unfair.
Death is the equalizer,
And All in Between is Magic, Light *and* Dark.

To this Mad Magician with fuchsia music
In his head, this multicolored god of Dance
Who moves my background to the lighted stage
In Aileyesque images of royalty
And lets it bow in front of me.

For Alvin Ailey

The Impresario's Promise

In this box
is a gem
of unimaginable beauty.
Eyes that choose
to see it
lose themselves
in amazement
and never
quite recover.
It opens your
mouth
and your
heart.
Beauty
unheard of
in any other gem like it.
Tonight,
you will be a witness
(and a believer, too).
When music is heard
and the curtain rises,
lo and behold!
you will never be the same.

For Paul Szilard

Opening Night: The "Getting Ready" Overture

New York City/ Month of May/ Midweek/ Mid-afternoon
And the music is rapid fast
Churning to the fast-frame movie movements
Of the people getting ready…

1.
Back from lunch an hour late
Mayreetha Hunt has bought out Saks.
Places her boxes out of sight,
Resorts the afternoon work.
Pile Number One goes first.
Pile Number Two. Pile Number Three.
And time out for the nails.
To the bathroom mirror with the new lipstick
And to think on that bad new dress under her desk,
Lying in wait to make its debut on the world.
Hers. To turn all heads
Tonight at Ailey. "Too much!" she cries.
Five o'clock/ through the revolving doors!
Onto the street/ up Fifth Avenue/ headin' across town!
To the music that is rapid fast
Churning to the fast-frame movie movements
Of a fast and pretty colored girl
On her way home to call Michael Tee
On her way home to get ready…

2.
And Señor and Señora Rodriguez
Are getting ready.
There will be no sitting down to dinner tonight.
There will be no hurrying home to watch the news.
No one will stop over to laugh and talk.

The Señora will merely draw the blinds
And ready the house for rest,
And Señor will clean the car and come inside.
Red boutonniere,
Jacket of pressed white linen,
And a gown in queen's black
Wait like two prize seats in the *orchestra*.
Nothing will make them change their plans.
Nothing will make them late…
While the music that is rapid fast
Churns to the fast-frame movie movements…

3.
And Rasheen and Peaches
Are getting ready.
Even though they are just getting up
From the night before.
"Get up, Rasheen. The sun is almost down.
I'm going to the cleaners. You spread the bed around.
I'm picking up my two-tone red and pink.
You take the dishes off the sink.
I'll get us something to eat from *Luigi's Cup*
I'm on *my* way out the door. *You* get up!"

"Peaches oughta be shame o' herself
Runnin' to everything like she do.
Now don't get me wrong, understand,
But two nights in a row?
I mean like hey! I like to party, too.
Las' night we hit the Village.
I mean like they was/ not/ read/ dee/ fo'/ us/ ba/ bee!
Don't get me wrong, understand.
I mean like, I mean like
They be into a casual thang downtown,
And me and Peaches be wearin' Pierre Cardin
And Halston to the bone!
They thought we was movie stars
Out on our own.
We smiled and said we just popped in
To say hello to Lena
Shake hands with Stevie
Give our love to Dionne
And congratulate Billy Dee.
Dusted busted and disgusted
We got home this morning at eight.
By the time we got to sleep it was ten.
Now it's almost six,
And Peaches talkin' 'bout these tickets she got
To go see this cat named Alvin Ailey *dance*.
Two nights in a row?
Now don't get me wrong, understand…"

4.
And Mr. and Mrs. Spurlock
Are getting ready.
Her dress is on the closet door.
His tuxedo is on the bed.
Gloves. Shoes (shined). Keys. And mints.
And soft spare handkerchiefs to wipe the tears
When daughter dances tonight.
And they will bring food for The Gala,
Brewed out of their tender good wishes.

"Back the car up to the kitchen door
And load on the baked hens stuffed
With country dressing and giblet gravy.
Find the candied yams in lemon sauce.
Here are the English peas and onion pearls.
That is pineapple upside-down cake
Topped with cherries and pecans.
These are baked hams glazed in brown sugar
And here is a tuna casserole
Of mushrooms, sweet cream and butter.
A bubbling potful of blackeyed peas,
Ten batches of cornbread,
And a vegetable medley garden fresh
For those who don't eat meat.
Last, the consommes broths and soups,
Iced tea cocoa coffee and lemonade,
Nectars pastries teacakes and puddings."
Backstage, under friendship's light,
White Yellow Red and Brown alike
Will feast on collard greens tonight
Around a cornucopia overflowing
And saucer'd with a Black love.

5.
And Miss Thing
Is getting ready.
Lover reads a list of things to do
And opens the door to their one-room
Haven: full of intimate things
And ruffles/ and flourishes/ and *eau de toilette*.
Full of Broadway show songs,
Full of bold, impudent love.
"Make sure the size of my hose
Is Large and Extra Tall.
Make sure the cobbler reinforces my heel
(A girl in size 11's can't afford to trip).
Make sure you bring my Revlon
And make sure you hurry back."
Who will Miss Thing pretend tonight?
Thumbing through her dresses, she hears
The children screaming, "All right, Miss Thing, girl!"
As she arrives as Ruby Dee.

Maybe she ought to go as The Beautiful Liz
And flash her fans with natural glamour.
Maybe she'll surprise them and be Diahann Carroll.
But with her new wig she could surely
Sling as much hair as Cheryl Tiegs.
Who will you be, Miss Thing, tonight?
Dina Merrill in pearls?
La Monroe in no underwear to make them gasp?
Or will you be a queen, or baroness?
Hurry back, Lover.
Kiss-ee kiss-ee and smack-smack
Right in front of the door.
And the music that is rapid fast
Churns…

6.
And the Alvin Ailey American Dance Theater *staff*
Is getting ready.
Not now said the morning stopping the alarm
Not now said the man going into the bathroom
Not now said the woman eating her oatmeal
Not now said the boy counting his money
Not now said the girl opening her address book

Not now said Bill Hammond checking his schedule
Not now said Carey King checking his budget
Not now said Meg Gordean writing another line
Not now said Edna Jones writing another order
Not now said Ed Lander opening his briefcase
Not now said Philip Laskawy taking another sponsor to lunch

Not now said the afternoon wiping a beer from its mug
Not now said the man opening the box office
Not now said the woman hurrying back to work
Not now said the boy getting out of class
Not now said the girl leaving her hairdresser

Not now said Denise Jefferson, resting
Not now said Pearl Lang, thinking
Not now said Ellis Haizlip, kidding
Not now said Tom Stevens, eating
Not now said Eleanor Applewhaite, stunned
Not now said Walter Raines, leaving
Not now said the evening shaking out the cushions
Not now said Otis the Doorman opening the doors
Not now said the man saying good evening
Not now said Wade Williams explaining it again
Not now said the woman on the arms of two men

Not now said the boy looking for his seats
Not now said the girl opening her program
Not now said the choreographer of "Treading,"
Crossing her fingers

Not now said Jean Noble, acting hostess
Not now said Ruth Ellington, movie queen in dark glasses
Not now said the stage manager, calling places
Not now said the head usher, closing the doors
Not now said Anna Kisselgoff, opening her notebook
Not now said Stanley Plesent, whispering to the air
Not now said Joyce Brown, raising her baton
NOW! said Alvin Ailey, sighing

Dance Of The Seven Rhythms

She opens as a pair of castanets
on the fingers of night.
Her hips move like mixers.
Her feet hammer out an incandescent joy
and her hands shout, Yes Yes Yes!

She rises slowly from the floor
like a beautiful solo from
Mr. Bernstein's baton.
She is as fresh as morning.
As precise. As well-rehearsed.
And always as correct.
Her polished dance
is as clear as a voice
resonating from center-stage.
She is a grand piano.

She changes quickly into a rattle
and gives us a pretty fair shake.
For three whole minutes
her body becomes Rio de Janeiro.
We go to the carnival with her.

She is a tambourine
from the front porch of great grandmother
who, when she shook the shimmy,
danced the danger dust from the door
to remove all spells
and open up the air
to the birds of good luck.

She is a bell.
As clear as a cry.

She is a cymbal.
A rainstorm.
A sudden downpour.
We are caught
and we are glad.
We are happy to be drenched
by this lavish shower.
She is a master. And
illusion is her forté.
She closes as a drum.
Africa with new blood in its veins.
Long lost hope returned
from no farther away
than next door.
She calls us like the house
we grew up in.
We will return for the restoration.
We will have a revival
and build again.
We know what must be done.
We are the children of this place
and she is our guide.

For Judith Jamison

The Night You Danced At The Gala

For you
It must have been just another dance
You promised yourself
To do for the people
Once and for all
Tonight!
You knew the time was right
And everything in the world
Was in its rightful place.

For us
It was Art
And luck and sudden wealth.
Star in the stardust.
Lovemaking between God and Artist.
Witnesses we
To an act of passionate grace—
God lives!
"And He can live in me, too."

For Miguel Godreau

Intermission

The interval came upon us
Like the sun from behind a cloud
And revealed our bare hearts,
Contented as housecats.
Sight and sound slowly separated again
And Art, God's greatest hope for earth,
Let go our minds
To let us radiate and spread the word.
We, as happy a mix as rum and Coke,
Lifted our voices, excited as school days,
And spoke of Life. Art
Had brought us together.
We mingled, friendly neighbors,
And promised, once again,
To do better.

For Christopher D'Amanda

*"For all Black women everywhere—
especially our mothers"*

Cry

...After Mr. Ailey's Dance

I.

Cry for Miss Catherine Moseley
   who worked so hard for the corporation she turned white.

Cry for Ada Allen
   who was the whole army.

Cry for Flora Mae
   who strained all of her days.

Cry for Rashida Imiri Waleed
   who lost her mind at a Black Power Rally.

Cry for Betty.

Cry for Coretta.

Cry for Margaret Jean
   who threw herself into Lake Michigan
   for revenge.

Cry for Mrs. Till.

Cry for Miss Sarah
   who took the licks in her face.
And

Cry for Mary
   who fell for a sweet-talking man.

II.

Cry for Babette Moore
    who was a good girl on a dirty trip.
Cry for Clarinda Carter
    who was known as The Valium Kid
    until the day she was unloaded like a suitcase.

Cry for Jodiah Muldrew
    who lost her nose in the snow machine and her brain to a single-edge blade.

Cry for Billie.

Cry for Dinah.

Cry for Marcia
    who went to bed and never got up.

Cry for "Betty Red"
    whose heart turned as cold as a slice of bologna.

Cry for Miss Maudie Reeva
    who soaked her body and soul in Johnny Walker Red.
Cry for Teerie Taylor
    who took the northbound train to the end of the line.

Cry for Ona Mae Humphrey
    who *prayed* herself free.

Cry for "Sweet Thing."

    And, please,
Cry for Mary
    who had to postpone her escape.

III.

Cry for Miss Lydee
    who never looked the devil's way.

Cry for Miss Esther
    whose bosom buddies were books.

Cry for Barbara Jordan
    who knew what it took.

Cry for Miss Gracie
    who survived the jump from a runaway train.

Cry for Mrs. Chisholm.

Cry for Aretha.

Cry for Leontyne.
Cry for Angela.   (Remember?)

Cry for The First Black Miss America
    who will say, "*it wudn no big thang.*"

Cry for Louise Beavers.

Cry for Dorothy (Dandridge).

Cry for Mrs. Glover
    who went to bat for a starry-eyed poet

Cry for Ntozake
    who braved Broadway for colored girls only.
Cry for Nikki.

Cry for Shalimar Lewis
    who rented a printing press
    and rolled her own.

Cry for Miss Gwendolyn.

Cry for Martha Mae Matthews and her sister,
    the one they call "Sweet Marie,"
    who "kept they bidness to they sef."

Cry for La Belle
    who said "it's just an all-girl band
    dealing with the facts and the pain."

And, yes,

Cry for Mary
    who gave birth to a poet.

Cry "for all Black women everywhere—
    especially our mothers."

* For Judith Jamison*
And for all those other dancers who have had to remember it all.
And, of course, for Mr. Ailey

Wade In The Water, Children
(From "Revelations")

The long, tree-limbed woman
with the white parasol
dances along the edges of the rivers
where her grandcestors
celebrated their love for each other
when they were enslaved
to the land where the rivers ran;
where victorious testimony
circled a chain of human bondage
and blessed the air and sky
in ceremonial release;
where forgiveness was asked
even for their captors.
The woman with limbs as long as a tree
beckons with her white parasol,
conceals our precious spirits
under the cover of her love
and guides us back to the place
where unity was celebrated
for survival;
where our forebears' hope
was phrased in hands and feet
where they privately kept
the customs of the tribe
and danced.

For Judith Jamison

Mothercountry

The sun nestles in the arms of a shadow
And evening falls across the land
Like the sweep of a magician's cape.
Three men appear in phoenix headdresses,
Their hard bodies half clad as earth,
Their formal drums locked inside their legs
Like fortresses. The drum is their defense,
Their voice.
It is
The message of the tribe. And they speak
As One:
We who were the Beginning still are.
Go not too far from me my children.
The dark ruby blood in your veins
Are the rivers from which Refinement sprang
We who were the Chosen still are.
The drums become a Warning
And stop.

And *She* appears.
Mothercountry.
Splendid as a flock of birds.
Her body feels the sound of new drumming,
Her feet meet the ground
And the ritual begins.
She smiles and stars blink.
She opens herself up to Us
And asks if we remember
And we say yes, we see, we know.

The rhythm of the drums slows
And her body contracts with pain.
It remembers the babies lost to the sea
Water that took them and diluted them.
Her arms and fists remember.
And so do the mournful drums.
Her eyes look into ours and say

We who were born of Peace
Have had to fight to keep it.
Her proud head
Leans back into the throbbing
And turns to the East.
The drums pulsate like hearts.
She turns to the West.
One beat faster
To the North and back
To the
South,
All over this world
The fight is still on
And he or she who would carve
A place to live
Must first be brave enough to fight.
The message of the tribe is clear: Be brave
Or be trampled with other fearful, helpless things.
Body hands and feet, arms legs and drums
Agree.

And Dance is born of joy,
Undulating syncopating activating Dance!
The drums deliver the message, and,
Mothercountry,
Tired from lashing understanding upon the world,
But grateful for her wisdom,
Dances.
Mothercountry,
Earth jewel and parent of Love,
Dances.
And We
Are re-captured.
Re-moved.

For Pearl Primus

Come Dance The Juba Looney
A Southern Black Dance Of The 1930's

And Prezell walked over to his Mattie Bee
Once again in this creaky
One-big-room of a building
Made of wood and love
And filled on this Christmas Eve Night
With people who have known each other
All their lives, and said,
May I have this dance?
May I have this dance for the last time
May I have this dance, Miss Pretty?

Not while you keep flirtin' out the corner your eye,
Prezell Creer.
Maybe, one day,
I'll dance a slow, slow looney with you,
Or do a fast little tooney with you.
Wear my hair up, twirled in a comb
And dance 'til night turns to silk white dawn.
Oh, I'll dance the Juba Looney with you,
Mister Creer, but
Not while you keep flirtin' out the corner your eye
And
Not while you got rovin' on your mind.

Dance with me, my chocolate sweet.
Dance with me, my pea.
Won't you stand and take my hand?
We'll dance until we're free.

Oh, my sweet Miss Mattie Bee,
I've given up flirtin' I've given up roamin'
I've given up teasin' too.
In my Sunday shoes shiny and black
In my suit of navy blue
I've come to dance the Juba Looney
And I ain' gon dance it with nobody but you.

Mattie Bee stood up and bowed
Like a proper young colored girl.
But something else had hold of her body.
Something else had hold of her tootsies.
It was that ol' African rhythm
Done come back to claim its own
And keep them New Country ways from
Moving in and takin' over the neighborhood heritage.
Something Else had hold of her, her, her.
Her head was a spinning record.
Her body was a needle.
Her heart Her heart Her heart
Beatin' like that
And so loud, too,
Since Prezell done come touched her hand
Like that,
And why are these people lookin' at me
And this ol' African rhythm
Done come back. Done come back, back, back.

Mattie Bee, daughter of Christians,
Forgot about the ways of white folks,
Forgot about Mama Sallie and the cryin' of Daddy John,
Forgot about Beora and Lafayette and Eddie B.
And Aunt Liza and Uncle Lonnie
And broke down in-
To a natural born black boogie woogie looney.
Let me go! she cried, like a trapped bird,
On this Christmas Eve night.
On this Christmas Eve night
While a poet child waits in Mary's belly.

Oh I'll dance a Juba Looney with you,
Prezell Creer,
I'll even dance you a looney in three-quarter time,
But
Not while you flirtin' out the corner your eye, and
Not while you got rovin' on your mind.

For Prezell and Mattie Bee Creer

Commentator

His dances are born to tell.

They review life like a critic,

Pointing out the blows—

Who made them

And why

And if we are better off.

He is the chief editor

Turning good deeds and atrocities

Into art

For us.

Dance is his demonstration,

His "March On Washington"

With signs that read

"Power to the people" and

"Love one another."

For Talley Beatty

Dance A La Eleo

Over there
in that corner   something dark
going up & down
like a passionate
storm cloud

Back there
on the other side   is green, the
color of an army

Down here   is black,
halo'd in white
with its arms
outstretched

Down there   navy blue
huddling
like two foot-
ball players

In the middle   orange spins
like cotton candy

On the sides   feet
and a red
handkerchief

And over here,
right here,
Something burning

For Eleo Pomáre

"Sounds In Motion"

It's how you hook up what you see
   with what you hear.
He is a saxophone
   a cool winner in his latest love.
She is a viola
   pleased and purring in her second fiddle role.
Those three are woodwinds
   waiting on the corner for evening.
He is a trumpet
   a local politician, blaring his heart out.
They are trumpets, too,
   with muted attitudes,
   charming their way through the crowd.
She is a lady trombone
   in pants and flat-heeled shoes,
   looking around for some action.
She is a piano
   stuck up *and* interested, bass clef *and* treble clef
   at the same time, a major chord.
He is a drum
   full of life (and hope)
   full of hope (and life),
And *she* is the conductor, the key arranger
   of their simultaneous and abstract expression.

For Diane MacIntyre

The Director-Choreographer At Work On A Musical Play

Straight
From the great wooden halls
Of his ancestors
He came with a banner and a horn.
And in the name of all that is royal
And Black
He laid the plan before them
And said, "*You* will be this one. *You*
Will be that one"
Until the blood in their bodies
Warmed.
Then he took the words
Of the poet, put them into the mouths
Of these people players
And told them to move.
"Taste the language
And remember Miss Flora. Miss Minnie.
And Miss Molly.
Remember Edward Lee:
'Mister' to you. 'Uncle' to some.
'Brave' to many. 'Man' to few.
Remember. Then move on. Here we go…"

And he led them to the rooms
That grandmother kept for company.
To the breakfast nook of hot biscuits and syrup,
Honeysuckle springs, Cashmere Bouquet talcum powder,
Dances on Saturday night, and Sunday shoes.
"Remember. Then move on. Here we go…"

And he led them to the grounds
Where Mailou danced,
Where the earth waited for
Jubilant feet and hearts made of hope
And rhythm descended from the crowns
Of Black thrones.
"This ground is sacred.
The shameless and the proud dance here.
Remember. Then move on. Here we go…"

And he led them to the songs.
"Catch these melodies on your voice
And raise them high enough for
The great wooden halls to hear
That the children have not turned
Around and lost the faith."

Now, art would be born on a stage
Like words on a page.
Directions, born out of his belief
In the common laws of culture,
Guide the players up the road, toward the goal.
"The melody shortens the march.
The song lightens the step.
Remember. Then move on. Here we go…"

For George Faison

Ode To A Dancer
(For Carmen De Lavallade)
after "Portrait of Billie"
choreography by John Butler

A woman,
A live ivory nude
With snake-slick hair
And lampblack eyes
And plums for cheeks
That match a scarlet mouth,

Slides into a sweep of satin,
Pearly white as moonstone,
And transforms herself into
Billie Holiday, that tragedy
To which no writer could have ever
Given birth.

A leg peeks out of a slit
And the saga of ruination begins.
Legs in white satin calling themselves
"Miss" cannot stay innocent for long.
A man appears,
Vague as night around a fire.
He is The Representative of No Good,
Pretty Eyes with no feeling,
A one-dimensional two-timer
Timing the time it takes to tilt her.

The fall is not all
In vain. Sometimes she breaks it
Long enough to come back with a gardenia
In her hair and sing about it, but
The pain is too much for Nice Guys.
We are not flower thieves.

The dancer will not let up.
Life dances death.
She takes us further down
Past a heart that has fallen and broken
Over and over again like a repaired toy.
Past her hypodermic needle, half penis and half poison.
She is so good when her body sings that
We enjoy the artificial moonlight, too.
Past the fallen songbird herself
All the way down to pride, that human steeple,
Which falls just before the body does.
We hold on for the crash…

When, suddenly, we remember
That we are watching a dance
And spring to our feet,
Clapping our hands like thunder.
We were under a spell.
"Encore!"
We want to go back.
"Encore!"

Stage Door Johnny

You can find him there
most every night at the door where
the magicians pass,
no more immortal now than he is,
but still stars, still divine, and
still the most beautiful among earthlings.

Out of costume, they are still his lords
and ladies, his chiefs and commandants,
dispensers of pulchritude and polish. And pride.
He is as thankful as a hymn
and shows his devotion with love tokens:

Tonight, his arms are two brimming rows of flowers,
mementoes for demigods and goddesses
(each of whom he knows by name).
He waits at the door for them
to experience their bloom and brilliance close up.
This is the part that is everlasting.

For Johnny H. Allen

Donnie o'

Donnie of the tradition

Donnie of the custom

Donnie of the disciplines and drills

Donnie of the dream

Donnie of the Muses

Donnie of the horns and flutes

Donnie of the drums and the hurdy-gurdy

Donnie of the flying notes

Donnie of the deepness

Donnie of the roses

For Donald McKayle

Falco

Is a pepper

Is a smooth green bell

Looking sweet

Or

Is a hot relish

A cayenne challenge

Looking for a dance

That is man enough.

For Louie Falco

Mama To The Dance

She thought she'd better take it in.
It was still young enough to need nurturing
And there had to be some way to make
Its big eyes happy. So,
She took it aside and made a deal with it.
She would love and care for its needs
If it would agree to go into training
And abide by all the rules.

Talent and Discipline wrestle like two strong men.

Soon, dance had turned into a big thing.
It was ready for the world.
She polished it in one or two places
And bought it a new coat,
Gave it a thermos of hot chocolate and her last
Twenty dollars
And sent it out to beautify the world—

Who thanks now this mother
For her gift.

For Louise Roberts

The Dance

I am newly born.

I am a seasoned kicker.

I am abandoned.

I am found.

I am a clean spot by the side of the road.

I am a tent.

I am a platform in the public square.

I am a hall.

I am an ad in the newspaper.

I am the color of excitement.

I am all the music.

I am flesh and blood.
I am the dance.

For Rael Lamb

The Conductor

He turns his majestic head around
From the days when he had
More than enough ideas to go around;
From the days when glory poured forth
In abundance from his pen,
Accustomed to writing into the night
On an empty stomach.
He turns his best side to
A hungry audience that screams
More! More! A thousand times more!

He does not hold back
But gives us only what we deserve.
He turns his great head around
From the lean years
From the days when "No" could almost kill.
He turns his strong and learned head away
From his music for only a moment now
And bows, lightly,
To the fickle applause
Of ol'...Broad...way!

For Howard Roberts

Maestro

Shhhh, God silences.
An artist has come to give us
Communion. And all must be
As quiet as rest stops
As he conducts His work.
He addresses the podium, his pulpit,
Like a reverend. And the musicians,
His priests, prepare to serve.
In the split second before he begins,
Love and poise join hands with his
And God stops time at a railroad crossing
To allow this mighty preaching to pass.

For Leonard Bernstein

"Brother John"

From a small stage in Mississippi
He came with a bag of songs
And a voice to deliver them in.

First comes his blues journey.
The story is sung on a voice made of pine.
Its sound never died with great grandfather.
We listen like children
And go back to the levee

To hear the songs of stubborn life.
His voice, so big in its painful beauty,
Turns and twists until despair vaporizes
And is burnt away by hope, that human sun;

Hope built on faith in an infinite wisdom.
Faith in goodness and justice, the songs recall,
Is always the rail you hold onto
To get through the journey.
His voice,
As sure as a priest's,
Paves the way.

For Brother John Sellers

Belafonte

Maybe in Paris or Portugal,
This word that is a name, that is a title,
Comes from seeing
Beautiful fountains
And shining streams.
Maybe in Puerto Rico or Palermo,
This combining form
That is a proper noun, that is a promise,
Has ample to do with
Waterfalls and ripples.
Maybe, in whatever city or whatever country,
This heading that is a surname, that is an epithet,
Has plenty to do with
Rushes
And billows
And surges
But in the United States,
This name that is an appellation, that is a word of honor,
Has most to do with
Splashes!
Splashes made
From the Broadway stage
And on the technicolor screen.
Splashes made
In the big cities
And on college campuses.
Splashes made
In the White House
And in *front* of the White House.

Splashes made
To cool
To warm
To shake hands
To love.
Yes, maybe, somewhere
In a different part of the world,
In the heart of some lovely province,
Or on the outskirts of some great metropolis,
This expression that is an interjection, that is a person,
Comes from seeing
A brawny beautiful fountain;
But here—
Here in the United States,
We see
Royalty.
Belafonte! American Royalty.
All in one line!

For Harry Belafonte

Life Dances

You are
A ball
A hop
A stage
And a play with music.
Terpsichore,
Our Muse of Dancing.
Our delight.
Our excellent review
And *divertissement*.
You are
An architect
Building scenes with bodies,
Structures
With human expressions
Across their faces,
Each a dissertation of life. Soulscapes.
Artist at work,
Generator,
Star of our lives
And theirs.

For Vera Lewis Embree

It Was A Cold And Dark And Dreary Night

It was a cold and dark and dreary night,
And there came a rap rap rapping at the door.
"The Lord is my shepherd," prayed Mama Sallie.
"Get the shotgun!" cried Miss Dill.
"Turn out the lights!" shouted Uncle Ray.
"Call the law!" ordered Miss Inez,
    still seventy-five and going on fifty
    and still ready for love.
"Lock the door and call the law!"
    cried this old wilted bride-to-be.
And the rain began to pour
Into the huge well
Of midnight blue.
And there came a shadow upon the light
That fell across the big and shaking
Pretty picture window.
"Oh, the end has come!" cried Mama Sallie.
"Lord, let me live just once before I die!"
    begged Miss Inez.
The key slid into the lock.
"Raise the ax!" pleaded Li'l Sister to Uncle Ray.
All was silence.   Until "Boom!"

The sound of laughter e
    choed-choed-choed
Down the trail of the lonesome night.
Then a big white smile came
    through the door.
"Girl!" scolded Miss Dill,
    recognizing her.
"Oh, it's you," drooped Miss Inez.

"I'm going back to sleep,"
    she said with the rest
Of what was left of her voice so low.
    "Wake me
When my bridegroom comes."
"You almost got yourself shot!"
    cried Miss Dill.
"You crazy child!"
Then Li'l Sister sighed,
    "Put down the ax, Uncle Ray.
It ain't nobody but
    Miss Luella's little girl, Vera,
Practicing her dances again."

For Vera Lewis Embree

Valley Of The Shadow

We went with you
On your journey to the burial ground
To inter the loved one you had lost.
At the sound of the passing bell,
Your look turned us into
A sea of sympathy.
Our hearts were open caves
Where you could have hidden.
We would have taken you in like a winded traveler,
But grief is a narrow house
And must be borne
Like hot weather or freezing cold.
A muffled drum helped you keep
Time in the dead march.
When the pain broke your stride
We left our seats to go and prop you up.
Your arms and legs wailed
Against the Creator.
No, no, we whispered, saner than you.
No, no, whining in an ancient but familiar chant.
We listened to the mourning dove's requiem
And bequeathed our faith to one another.
God's acre trembled.
Your performance brought us
All the way to the edge.
And, yea, though we walked through
The valley of the shadow,
We held on.
Praise be.

༄ *For Alana H. Barter* ༄

From the dance, "Elegy," Choreography by Vera L. Embree

Star Pupil

The floor is where the dance lived.
It was a table for the feet.
It could be worked on like hands.
Feet, instead of hands, would find the steps
To make the dance come true; to
Get it up off the floor and give it life.
You were as sharp as a tool.
She was a carver.
Your feet were in her hands.
Mathematics would help her out.
Foot-stomping substituted for a drum,
And soon a dance was up and moving.
The floor was the canvas upon which it sat.
You were the color and texture on top of it all.
She watched like a new mother.
You were the show.
She was your reason for coming.
You were her reason for staying.

For Andrea Brown ... protégé of Vera Embree

Movement

Music to our eyes

A tune dancing before us

An air upon the air

A sonata glowing in starlight

A serenade for sight

A concerto for legs

A carol in costume

For Carol Morisseau

Pastorale

Leaving our debates
  and wars of words
    frictions
      scrambles
        (tugs
          &
            pulls)
              just outside

The door (like wet galoshes)
We tiptoed
Into the place
Where the musicians
Were about to
Hold forth,
Skilled as machinists
With their instruments
And as talented as thrushes
With their tone colors.
Their reputation for memorable performances
Had pulled us over like a patrolman.

And not since it rained in Aunt Flora's garden
One summer dry spell

And not since the taste of
Your first candy apple

And not since your first ride
On a ferris wheel

And not since a girl or a boy
First smiled especially for you

And not since the first time you were grand
Had there been music like this:

Lifelines
For stranded, weathered spirits.

 *For James Byars Family*

The Best Music You Ever Laid Your Ears On

Brother,
The day we heard you were coming back
There was a band waiting for you
Up the street, around the corner,
Out of the way, so that the mossbacks
Could not hear the air tuning up
Could not see the streets filling
And women's tears welling
From joy. It was the place
Where we used to meet you in the afternoon,
Our tired suns ready
For your settings of topaz atonement,
Where you made music to our souls
And turned us on, and turned us on…
Until we became night lights,
Full of Black satisfaction
And love enough to love everybody.

For Frankie Crocker, WBLS, and the year, 1975

Disco Ritual: Circa 1976

Last night—
Missing you since you went away,
She went out.
Last night
She tried to dance you
Right out of her life!
She joined the others
At the place where
Love, Lost and Found,
Testifies to Joy and to Pain.
Last night
She wanted to prove that she
Could be happy without you, so
She went out
And gathered with the tribe.
She stepped onto the dancing ground
And worked her way upwards
Toward the Light.
Her spirit began to move
With the drum,
And she grabbed the middle
Of the rhythm and held on!
Her arms flew into the air
And she thought she saw
Her great grandmother
As a young woman
Building a house!
She touched the hands of others
Reaching up through the darkness
For the Light,
And there in her space place
Of the tribal ground
She forgot about you—
And became Alvin Ailey!
She straddled a black magnificent steed
And rode it bareback
Across the lightning sky—
And she was Saint Joan!
Motion stirred in her hips,
Curving around the center
Of her space place, and she remembered
Central High School, that time when
She fell into the senior prom
Driving a chariot
And was hailed by the crowds!
She waltzed to a red jazz violin
And smiled as Nicolo Paganini
Played on.
She stood in the lobby of the theater
At intermission and everybody whispered,
"There she is!" again.
She heard the music ask the tribe
If they felt the spirit,
And the tribe cried, yes, yes!
At the tops of their voices,
Thank you!
Cure us!
Make us whole again!
We have brought our Joy and
Our Sorrow to your altar—

Robértu Ras Riley

Purify us!
She climbed up among the stars,
Wrapped her long legs around a meteor—
And she was Wonder Woman
Laughing her way across the top
Of a midnight rainbow!
When the music got too hot,
She blew herself over a snowfall,
And she saw Poor Beulah, The Maid,
Dancing outside of her tomb
With a broken headstone in her hand!
Honor our Pain!
The drum rolled,
And she fell down a red velvet road
To the gates of Hell
And licked her tongue out at the Devil!
She borrowed Time from her grandfather
And stopped the clock!
Behold our Joy!
Purify us, and let us in!
And the members reached up
And caught the Light
And swallowed it
With their souls!
And she became all of her ancestors at once!
They stepped into Heaven
And danced like they never had before!
The spinner crowned their heads
With circling, spiraling light
And turned his music
Into their bodies

And made Love to them,
And they cried, yes, yes, yes!

Then, the last music played
And she looked among the tribe
For someone to carry home from Heaven.
She saw only your old friends
Locked into each other's arms
In this final music ecstasy,
A Lover's Choice.
She saw Antonio shaped into a beat.
She saw Lisa and Diego
Looking into each other's souls.
She saw Tyrone and Marty
Heading toward a reverie.
…And when the last strain of music
Had floated away on the wings
Of the North wind,
She came down from Heaven.
And when the last coats had been picked up,
And the last telephone numbers given out,
And the last looks on the faces
Of the merely hopeful had been, finally, exchanged,
She walked away from the dance ground
Where she had tried to forget you
And stepped back onto the familiar streets
Of her New York City—
Where she knew you were, someplace,
Walking home with someone new.

Antonio et "Le Jardin"

He stands,
   at first, watching.
Then he conducts
   from the sidelines.
He moves like a hawk
   excited about this
   new prey he has
   channeled and carved
   with the looks
   of his one tweed suit.
He is not afraid to bring
His Lower East Side
To Midtown Manhattan.
He knows now
   what the language is.
He camouflages his garlic
   with proper mints.
Once, he only dreamed
   of dancing here,
   comfortable in his suit
   and unafraid.

Tonight, he has discovered
   that Midtown has merged
   with the rest
   of his world.
Tonight, his "Hustle"—spun
   from the souls of men
   and women who give birth
   to Dance—brings new life
   to "Le Jardin" where everything
   is more than beautiful.
Tonight, in this new Midtown
   Foliage,
He knows
   that his "once-questioned" Latin
More than fits.

For Antonio Rodriguez
"Le Jardin": the "in" discotheque on Manhattan's eastside.

Matinee Idol

What must your world be like
Macho Matinee Idol
So much of all the fabric
That makes the city up.
We know you haven't gotten where you are
Without having worked hard
Without having sacrificed
And taken the bullshit.
It has made you "professional"
And we like the way it looks on you.

I see you on the subway sometimes
With a woman on each arm
And I smile and say *Ummm*
And you smile and say *Ummm*
And we go our separate ways.
But what if we got together
One o' these times and
Swung buddies?

You could be my partner for a day
Be my crony for an evening
Be my chum be my pal
And I'd be your sidekick for a time
Your comrade your ace boon coon.

We'd be allies
Be Pylades and Orestes
Be North America and South America
Be Hector and Robert
Be for real.
Ask one of your ladies along and we could
Be the Three Musketeers.

You and I and Me and You
Could swing buddies
Could swing buddies/buddies/buddies.
We could turn on the Isley Brothers
And get into their slow drift.
I could make an Indian fire pudding
And you could bring the wine.
I could set the stage
And you could dress it.
One day,
More glorious than new jewels,
We could swing buddies.
Me and You and You and Me
Could swing buddies
Could swing buddies/buddies/buddies.
Me and You and You and Me
Could swing buddies.

For Hector Mercado

Star Dance

Not since I saw Jeremiah dance

The Hoochee Koochee

And Aunt Florence the Dip

And Uncle Jeems the Jump Back

Have I seen the Boogie Woogie

Danced like you danced it

Under the light of my morning star dream.

The trees rocked like old smiling grandfathers
And your dance signaled the dawn.

For M.S. Brown

Cake Walk

Don't dance over there all by yourself.
Come over here and dance with me.
First we'll execute a quick trick-step
Like the ones they used to do for a nickel.
Then we'll do a fast front-front
A side a side and a front-front fast,
Half-turn slow motion rigmarole!
We'll reach down to the middle of the 60's
And drive the crowd wild with some
High-stepping side-tripping temptin' Temptations
And wind all the way back up
To the mighty Mighty Dells!
Last, we'll add a rockin' organ
And a snarlin' spittin' harmonica.
Don't dance over there all by yourself.
Come over here and dance with me.
Let's slide our feet across
This walkin' talkin' boogie
And take the cake!

For M.S. Brown

Joan Of Art

"An engraving on the crowd,
the blurred crowd."
—Gwendolyn Brooks

Print
Of beauty,
Picture
Of the grand style,
A fresco
Of coolness.
Pencil drawing
Of a cartoon,
A panorama
Of spirit.
A portrait
Of romanticism,
And a composition
Of the boogie woogie.

For Joan Sandler

On The Road

Since you have been away
The world has come to an end
And begun again for me.
My nerves even turned to steel once
And I went down into my grave
And stood there and laughed
For still above me were the stars
And a vision of Pollyanna
Offering me the crown from her head.
Since you have been away
I have come *that* close to
Having my star discovered
And framed in the universe.
I have reached past distracting poverty
And beyond insanity
And touched the skirt-tail of Broadway.
With a child's heart and an open mouth
I have watched the shelter fall
From around me.
But I have not perished.
Miracles have kept me alive

To bring Jah's message to the world.
Since you have been away
I closed off that room
Where I used to go and find you
In a pile of brassy rhythm,
Red plumes, green life and laughter.
No need to keep a room open
That only you could fill.

No need to conjure magic
That only you could make.
No need to look from a room
Onto a street that turned into a road
That led to you somewhere out of sight…
All to do was leave a light
In the window and close the door
And hope that the road you were on
Was filled with smooth places
And the best of times
From each and every season.

For Alvin McDuffie

Life Dancers

The years pass like nobody's business.
Already it is tomorrow.
Soon it will be next year.
And next year we are old,
Satisfied as cats who have eaten until
They can't see,
Or raging like old jackals in the darkness,
Or silent breathing bodies with minds
As blank as deserts
Waiting in line with a number
To return to the dust.

And El Dorado will still lay out
Her welcome mat.
Detroit will still provide the world with
Wheels to go faster, faster.
San Francisco will still beckon like a lover.
Hollywood will still flash bodies like money,
And New York will still have the biggest stick.
And another of life's young dancers
Will come on the scene to do his number,

Thinking, as we did, that he has forever
In the palm of his hand.
And God save us all,
We hope.

For Alvin Ailey

Forever Yours

You lugged it all
From out the forest dark
And like a fragile Christmas madonna
Unwrapping colored stars
From thin tissue
You placed them high upon the tree
Hushed the world for their coming
And turned on the lights
With your love.

#

For Ivy Clarke

More Than "Just A Word Or Two"

"Inside" was the title that Ulysses Dove gave to the dance he created from a series of poems on Love that I had written especially for him and his new piece of choreography. I did not get a chance to see the dance until well after it had premiered at the Kennedy Center and had toured the country. I had read the reviews, however. Everywhere, the critics talked about the dance's "power," its "propulsive movement" and Ulysses' talent, his unique, original choreography. "But the poetry," they said, "while having some originality of its own, is fragmented and disjointed. The poet has only a limited understanding of what love is and, thereby, misses his opportunity to make a profound statement. His lines do not go anywhere and are ruinous to the dance." I was devastated. No one had ever said such things about my poetry before.

Finally, I was able to see the dance when it made its New York debut. The critics were right. I was shocked and disgusted. Ulysses had taken lines from one stanza of a poem and joined them onto another line from a different stanza! In at least two instances, he had used only one or two words from a line of poetry that could only be understood by hearing the whole line! Yes, the poetry was "fragmented." Yes, the poetry was "dilapidated" and "rundown." To me, it even made one particular section of the dance appear downright silly. I was, as they say, fit to be tied!

When I was, at last, able to see Ulysses and talk to him about it, he was aloof and defensive. He had his reasons, he said. "The words and lines I used were exactly applicable to the images I wanted to show." "But you have sacrificed the meanings of the poems!" I said. We fought. Alvin Ailey got into it. "Ulysses is young in the ways of literature," he said. "You're the teacher. Show him how 'out of gear' you think your poems are to his dance." (I can hear Alvin's wise, patient voice now.)

And, so, like hundreds of other students before him to whom I had taught English grammar, composition and literature, I had to "school" Ulysses. It was not as hard as I had thought. I read all kinds of poems to him, in all kinds of voices. I removed lines from stanzas and showed him how "out of context" a stanza can become when a line, or even a word, is taken from it. Ulysses, however, was more impressed with my *reading* of the poetry than he was with where the lines should go…After two or three such encounters, Ulysses saw the light and was "sorry." "I'm going to re-do 'Inside,'" he said later. "You will have total control over the poetry. And, this time, I will want you to be the narrator of the poems. Write some new ones for me. Next time, we'll hit 'em with a one-two punch!"

For years, Ulysses and I spoke about "the new 'Inside'" and how we would get together and revamp it. By now, Ulysses' career had taken off like a sprinter. Certainly, he had been well trained for it. Studying dance, in the beginning, with Carolyn Tate, Xenia Chilstowa, Jack Moore, and Judith Dunn, with Bertram Ross, Helen McGehee, and the great Mary Hinkson. Later, he studied with Maggie Black and Alfredo Corvino. He performed with José Limon, Mary Anthony, Pearl Lang, and Anna Sokolow, before joining the Merce Cunningham Dance Company in 1971, where Alvin Ailey saw him dance one evening and asked him if he would be interested in auditioning for his company. Ulysses was very interested. He joined the Alvin Ailey American Dance Theater and became one of its star dancers. He made his *choreographic* debut with the company in 1979 with his dance 'Inside.' The following year, after eight years with "The Ailey," he left to become the assistant director of *Groupe Recherche Choreographique de l'Opera de Paris*. He was there for three years and then moved on to other prominent choreography positions with other companies—abroad and in the United States. I would hear of him in Stockholm, in Frankfurt, in London. Once, he came home to New York in late 1989, the year Alvin Ailey died, and Ulysses and I met. He was pretty shaken up over the death of his mentor. "...I have a much deeper concept of Love now than I did ten years ago when we did our dance ("Inside"). Something happens to the body, too," he said, "when you lose someone to death. Ten years ago, I was mostly concerned with what happens to the mind; but the body becomes impaired, too. I hope you can come up with some poems about *that*. Alvin would love us for it," he said, both of us choking back tears. "I must find the time to re-work "Inside," Ulysses said.

After Alvin Ailey's funeral, Ulysses was gone again—pursuing his quest of the dance, collecting and selecting all of that private and individual data (the rhythm, the movement, the sound, the look) that choreographers need to make a dance—for whatever occasion and for whatever company. Time and inclination will determine what goes on next. Ulysses was very talented and popular and very much in demand. Soon, I would hear of him again from the world's capitals; then communicating with me once from Dallas, Texas, in 1993. He would soon return to New York and we would have "big fun" this time "working on *our dance to Love.*"

Four years would pass before I would hear of Ulysses again. The Ailey Company announced its 1997 season at New York's City Center Theatre. I noticed that in its brochure, the Company had planned special evenings for "the works of Ulysses Dove." I was very excited. I would be writing about the Company's new season for *American Performing Arts Review*. The highlight of my review would surely center around Ulysses' dances. I would attend the first evening of these "special performances." I wrote a note to Ulysses, telling him how happy I was that he was back in town and how I looked forward to our upcoming collaboration. I put the note in a small envelope, wrote his name on it and sealed it. I rushed into the theatre on the evening of December 7, 1997, and handed the envelope to the head usher. "Please send this backstage to Ulysses Dove," I instructed. About 10 minutes later, just as I had finished greeting some people I knew and just as I was about to go to my seat, the usher came back to me, her head down, "I'm sorry, Mr. Riley," she said, "but Ulysses Dove died over a year ago." I was stunned! Just as I was the last to hear about "Inside," I was the last to hear of its choreographer's death. I watched that whole evening's performances *"with heart fit to break,"* as Browning says in his poem. Lines from all the poems I had been selecting and collecting (my *own* "data") for our new dance raced through my head. I left the theatre talking to myself. Everybody wanted to know what was the matter with me. Everybody had such sympathy for me. Especially Miss Jamison, the Company's artistic director. I brought the envelope back home with me and placed it in my top desk drawer, where it has remained all these years. One day, I'll give it to Miss Jamison and ask her to open it and read it back to me.

And so, then, here are your poems, Ulysses. While they may be very much like the poems I might have written for "our new 'Inside'," they, instead, pay tribute to you—to your enormous talent, to your work, to your life and death, and to your everlasting joy.

— *R.R.R.*

"Ulysses, O, Ulysses!"

*A Tribute To The Late
Dancer/Choreographer
Ulysses Dove*

"Ulysses Dove, dressing room, 1975"
photo by Alfredo Quiles

"Ulysses, O, Ulysses!
Where do you wander tonight?
What new adventure do you encounter
On your journey home?..."

after Homer's epic poem

Dedications

For
Miss Judith Jamison
Who first danced my poetry
on the professional stage

For

Mr. Robert Ruggieri

Who first put music to it

For

President and Mrs. Jimmy Carter

and

Mrs. Jacqueline Kennedy Onassis

Who were in the audience

the night it premiered

The Kennedy Center

Washington, D.C.

1980

And for

Mr. Alvin Ailey

Who loved it all

To everything there is a season, and a time

To every purpose under the heaven:

A time to be born, and a time to die…

A time to weep, and a time to laugh;

A time to mourn, and a time to dance…

—from the book of Ecclesiastes

A time to be born...

Once Upon An Evening Star

There was a boy

There was a talent

There was a teacher

There was a sacrifice

There was a thin place

There was a will

There was a sign

There was an inspiration

There was a city

There was a company

There was a master

There was a dance

There was a dancer

There was a stage

There was an evening

There was a star

A time to laugh ...

Dance All Around

We know you *bad*.
You look good even in a minuet,
In a rigadoon or a fast junket.
You can turn a fandango
Into a bolero
With one move of your hips.
You can dance a polka and a jig and a fling,
Allemande or quadrille, don't mean a thing.
It takes finesse to flip through the air
Like a coin for all to see.
But just *how bad* are you?
We know you got the mettle for a morisco,
But have you got the guts for a kozotzky?

A time to die...

In Order For The Dance To Continue

No one is being introduced to anybody.
No one is shaking hands,
And no one has ordered another round of drinks.
No one is back and forth on the telephone to Chicago.
No one is making "Fourth of July" plans in Detroit,
And no one is taking a quick trip to Philly.
No one is conducting a meeting.
No one is throwing a party.
No one is giving advice,
And no lessons are being taught.
No one is laughing and smoking cigarettes.
No expert is speaking on the human condition,
And no corrections are being made.
No one is having dinner at a French restaurant,
And no one is making any toasts to anyone else.
No one is walking leisurely toward home,
And no one is reading any deeply moving poetry.
No one is telling someone else how wonderful somebody sounded
When they called from Hollywood.
No one has any high hopes for artists,
And no one is longing for them.
No one is sorry for having left someone.
No one is intellectualizing somebody else to death,
And no one is bullshitting himself by pretending.
No one has announced to someone
That they will never speak to them again.
There is no beautiful conversation going on at somebody's table,
And nobody is applauding at "The Ailey."
There is no music,
And there is no one on a one-to-one anything.

There are only people
looking at each other;
And a hole where one of us
just slipped through—
And a poet, like a scientist in a laboratory,
pacing the floor for words
to fill it up.

A time to weep ...

"A Time To Weep"

The body is out of hand.

It is a whirlpool.

The heart sinks.

There are no instructions.

This is a baptism in your own sweat.

You stay as quiet as you can

For as long as you can.

Then it strikes again:

You are dipped in tears.

This is "a time to weep!"

Your suffering cannot be decoded.

There is no morphine for your pain.

This storm must be borne;

And all you can do,

All you can ever hope to do,

Is "take the hit."

A time to mourn ...

Everything Here Is Black And Gray

Everything here is black and gray.

Writing a poem won't add color.

There are no similes because

nothing here is like anything else.

The hand on the clock has stopped

at a late late hour. Everything

is lifeless. Even my power to personify

the dead has vanished.

The only metaphor is sadness.

Hyperboles stand around waiting

for some action, but nothing moves.

There are no drums or trumpets;

no rhythm, except the breathing

in and out of a man sitting,

alone,

longing for a comrade.

A time to dance ...

Instrument

The rhythm plays on his bones
Like a mallet
Thudding against a drumskin.
He closes his eyes
And the beat plays around
The back of his head
And works its way down
Through the rest of him.
Rapture overrules his reason
And dance takes him over like a strongman.

His body longs and stretches
Like a blue chord.
It moves as quietly as a secret
Through the silence, a dark solo
Looking for company,
Looking for a piano, a mate
To swing with, to go round
And round with,
Be partners with.
(We remember when we wanted somebody, too.)

Then, discovering joy
In the pit of the picture he is making,
His mood switches, fast as a light.

The rhythm quickens
And runs up and down his body
Like fingers on the throat of a saxophone.
His arms become the entrance to Birdland.

His legs slide us through the crowd
To a table jammed against a bandstand.
We move to the edge of our seats.
A horn is alive and kicking!

#

Encore!

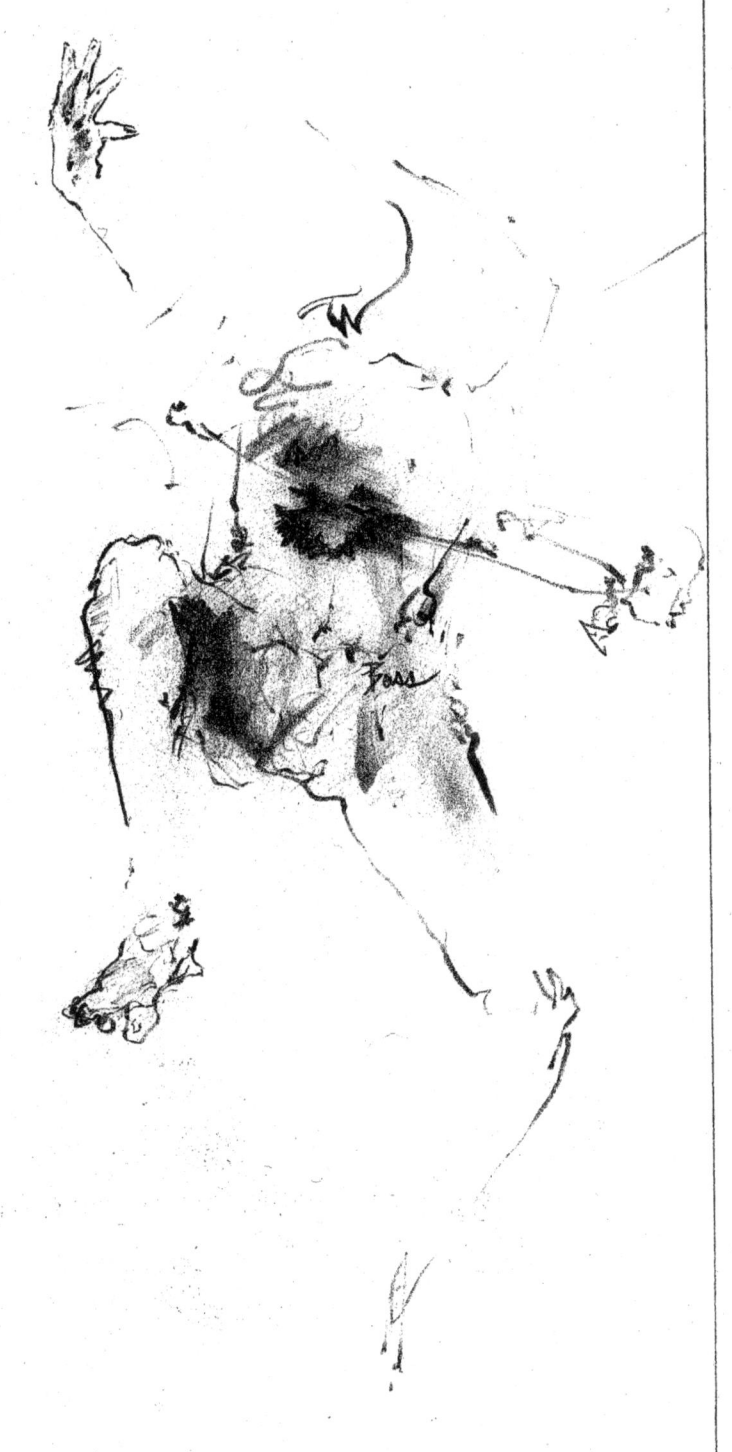

Ritual One:
Blackbox's Backbone

"Ritual One: Blackbones Backbone"

For Lowell Quentin Bass
…for his cover drawing

"Ritual One: Blackbones Backbone"

There was this poet and there was this artist.
They met on a college campus where the poet
Was carrying on as a grand professor
Of the dramatic arts and letters.

The artist, of senior classification
And honors as sterling as the USMC,
Saw the poet professor strut his stuff one night
And fell, as they say, madly in love with him.

Well, of course, the poet professor felt like he had
Been hit over the head with a ton of feathers.
They discussed Painting. And Music. And Dance. And Poetry.
Inspiration flowed between them like good luck.

Their minds locked. They were as classic as an urn.
And so they had like this spiritual marriage.
They didn't pitch a tent and have people over
Or anything as modern as that. It was private.

Just the two of them. And the gods.
It happened one night when the poet professor started
Talking about his new book.
"What's it called?" asked the artist.

"*BUM*," said the poet professor. "It's about this young man
Whose initials spell out the word 'bum'; and I want *you*
To do the cover." The artist shouted like a preacher.
"Good," said the poet professor. And they burned incense
And rejoiced.

The artist's drawing was no mere setting.
He captured the poet's theme like light.
One look and there was no such thing as words.
A picture had swallowed them all.

The book sold like women's dresses.
The small publisher paid off all his bills
And went out of business.
But the artist and the poet didn't mind.
They were a hit.
The poet professor quit his job and moved to Gotham.
The artist flew off to Hollywood for some quick money
And later joined the professor on Manhattan Island
For Christmas.

There, they swung through the buildings
Like monkeys through trees.
Happy as a hyena's sound, the subway
Was their laughing stock.

They absorbed life like sponges
And squeezed them out in their art.
In a year's time,
The poet-professor, now writer-director,

Had a comedy and a drama,
With sets designed by the artist,
Playing The Lambs Theater
On good ol' Off-Broadway.

They glowed like two nice heads of hair.
Manhattan, this old girl with her
Make-up in place, her ass in the wind,
And all her real teeth, was all right.

That is, until…
Until the night before the closing night
When the poet-professor-turned-writer-director-turned-nervous wreck
Turned and heard someone say,

"They've stolen all the money!"
And he (you know who), our trusting chameleon,
Passed out like somebody had unplugged him.
Life was as funny as hell…Later,
in the Exhaustion Room of the hospital,

The artist propped his friend's head up
And said he was leaving town.
He had a commitment to keep in Hollywood.
"But before I go," he said, "here is the drawing

To illustrate the book you're working on."
It was a picture of a man, that jester and wizard, dancing in spite of his pain and beyond it.
"It is how I see you," said the artist,
"As you work and wonder and wait."
"You recycle pain into fuel.
Life, for you, even at the bottom, is a dance.
Your attitude is a sermon.
This is the *real* life of Riley.

My drawing,
'Ritual One: Blackbones Backbone,'
Is a nudge at the world's shoulder.
It says, *Look. Here. Life Dances!*"

"Hurry back," said the *poet* professor,
And kissed the drawing
And pulled the covers back over his head
And cried and vowed

Never to go near a theater again.
He would concentrate on his writing.
He would sit on the side of his bed, he said,
For the rest of his days and write poems.

By Valentine's Day,
The poet-professor-
Turned-writer-director-
Turned-poet-poet,

Had succeeded in turning his one room
Into a gilded cage when the artist returned.
The artist had always known that the professor
Could recover from anything about as fast as you could pump

An inner-tube tire full of air,
But this was incredible.
Here the poet-professor was, grinning again,
And up to some new project already.

And *what's this*, the artist inquired,
As the poet-professor opened a tiny silver box,
Took a pinch of something out of it,
Put it behind his bottom lip and said,

"Snuff," with a look that asked,
And don't you think that's a nice thing to do?
Snuff? queried the artist, with his nose turned up.
"Snuff," said the professor, his voice, now, a
Seventeenth-century drawing room.
"All right!" said the artist.
Now he would have to endure *this*.
The poet-professor had taken to dipping snuff!
And although nobody cool today did such a thing,

At least it wouldn't be as bad as
The time the professor carried around
A bottle of blackberry brandy and took swigs of it
From under tables at restaurants.

Only once did the artist nearly complain.
There had been some talk of the poet-professor
Dressing up as The Bronze Marilyn Monroe
And meeting him at "21" for lunch.

Well, *that* he would never have been able to stand.
And just as he was about to say something,
The poet professor lost his nerve.
No. Snuff-dipping *wasn hardly no big thang!*

So they joined up again.
Members of each other's federation.
Manhattan rolled back the rugs,
And they went dancing with *les girls* at "Better Days."

Both were on their way to somewhere
And each as dumb as the other
And each as wise
And each lit a candle for each's dark.

A year went by like a man on a motorcycle.
One day the artist came running to the professor.
Someone had slapped him in the face.
Someone had demanded some reality from him.

"Screw all this fantasy bullshit!" they had screamed.
But the artist couldn't do that,
So he packed up all his reveries
("I'll go to Memphis," he said) and left.

"And I'll visit," said the sad poet professor.
The artist had always been his big, lovable bird,
Grounded, with big feet and unbending wings
That yearned like a farm boy to fly.

"I'll visit," he said,
And turned back to his poems, his safe place.
He seemed to be healing just fine these days
And he *wasn bout to break no stitches*.

But it took years of silence to heal.
Big daily doses.
No visits no calls no letters.
They remained as quiet as a library with each other.

The years had piled up
Like a big stack of old picture calendars
With all the freshness worn off
All the scenes of the recent past.

The professor,
Now a full-fledged poet,
Could, at last, do something about it.
You see, he had worked out a deal with the years.

They promised, if he would let them pass, the years,
By bending to their needs,
They would give him the strength to
Get to the *Land of Stardom*.

"Well, this is all well and good,"
He tells Diana, goddess of the moon,
And the only deity today
Who will listen to him talk about his dilemma.

Diana was the only goddess
Allowed to sit in on their dreams
In the first place
Back when...

Back when the world said no to enthusiasm
And you kept your dreams muffled
But your head up
Or you both went begging.

"O, Goddess of the Moon," laments the poet-poet,
"I must find my young friend of the beauteous grace,
My young virtuoso of the pencil,
'Ze Artist.'"
"I can't go to *Starland* without any color."
"Call him," said Diana. "Go to some high place
And call him. Call him at midnight on the next full moon,
And I'll plug your message into his mind."

"Moonstruck!" babbled the poet-professor
(Oh, he will *always* be a professor) on his way to
The George Washington Bridge.
There, he climbed to the highest point

And looked out over the mighty Hudson River.
"Come back!" he shouted.
"We'll go to *Starsville* and dance
The 'Hustle' again!

It is time to join up once more,
And the only way to get to *Starsplarz* is to fly.
Remember, I got the wings and you got the feet.
We'll *take* off from where we *left* off.

I'll read you a poem everyday.
O, come back to Gotham, Ace!
We'll marinate the George Washington Bridge
And eat this big mugghugg alive!"

#

Acknowledgments

To Peter Leroy Hall
To Robert McDonald Anderson
To Warren and Sheila Hanson
To Bruce and Phyllis Sachs
To Ellis and Victoria Bates

To Paul M. Ehrlich

To Wilton Woods

To Monière Noor

To James Huey and Elnora Smith

To Steve Karakashian

To Ronald Levandusky

To Rosendo Delano Altheimero
To Mel Embree
To Royal Cousins
To Ralph McCain
To Marcia McDonald
To Bruce and Beth Morrow
To Kwush and Saundra Steele
To Chardelle Imani
To Vincent Cianni
To Mark Rinis

To Ed Shockley

To Jórgé and Maria Villegas

To Andrzej Nikonorow

To Pete Sims

To Nile and Marzell Smith
To Savannah Frazier
To Laura Villegas
To Feddie and Bertha Moore
To Lamos and Julia Sturgis
To William Henry Burks
To Virginia Burks Green Smith
To Rosemary Brooks
To Ann Brown
To Buddy and Chris Furlough
To Patricia Bates
To Herbert Wilson

To Ida Jane Grace

To Melba Rose White

To George Franklin Cameron
To Grace Menzies
To Toni Moore
To Fannie Mae Gunn
To Sam and Ruth Frazier
To Bessie Moore

To Cynthia Scott
To Ronald Reel
To Scott and Carol Ellen
To Jane Wiley
To Dina Joyner

To Lee Allen and Juanita Torrence

To Georgia Fields McIntyre
To Ella Jean Briggs
To Irma Randall Jackson

To James Zell and Thelma Green

To Catherine Carter Blackwell

To Wallace A. Sims

To Robert L. Perkins

To Renauld White

To Bill Hammond

To Tee Schnugg
To Harold Youngblood
To Mary Hinkson
To Phil Diedrick
To Meg Gordean
To Walter Nicks
To Lois Framheim

To Chenault Spence

To Raymond and Nancy Rodriguez

To Gladys Antoinette Williams

To Mabel Johnson

To Tom Blewitt

To C. Wilmer James

To my mother, Mary
To my aunt, Gloria
To my uncle, Elzie B.
To my aunt, Dorothy
To my son, Patrick
To my cousins, Esther Louise,
Sammie Rozzell, Charles MacArthur,
Elzie and Frances, and Annette

To Renée Morgan
...Ailey's first archivist,
for her enthusiasm and dedication

And to Milli Stennis
...for introducing me to Alvin Ailey

Alvin Ailey American Dance Theatre performs legendary Alvin Ailey's Revelations in Miami's Adrienne Arsht Center for the Performing Arts.

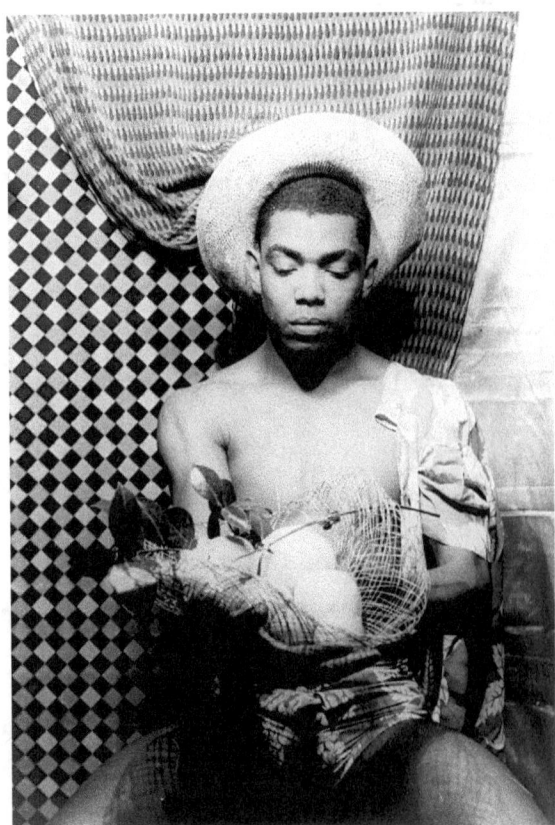

"Portrait of Alvin Ailey." 1955 Mar. 22. Creative Americans: Portraits by Carl Van Vechten, 1932-1964, Library of Congress.

Robértu Ras Riley...

Robértu Ras Riley writes poetry, plays, short stories, essays, and critical reviews. This is his third book of poems. Three of his plays have been produced at the famous Lamb's Theatre (Broadway and 44th Street) and the prestigious Theatre-of-the-Riverside Church, in New York City. His knowledge of mass communications, English, and speech and drama prepares him for his role as Artistic Director of the New York City Poetry Theatre, where he performs with the company. He is also chairman of The New Rastas, a social circle. He lives in Manhattan.

Alvin Ailey . . .

Photo by Susan Cook

Alvin Ailey and his troupe of seven dancers opened on the mainstage of the 92nd Street Y on Friday evening, March 7, 1958. That marked the first performance of Alvin Ailey American Dance Theatre anywhere. Alvin had a gift for making dances. From that moment on, the world was ready to receive him. For 31 years, he led his company to fame as its artistic director. His mission and vision never changed. The words he spoke that night in 1958 held true to the end of his life, on Friday, December, 1, 1989: "All I want to do is to say something about black culture. I want to have a black company similar to the folk companies that I have read about and seen in Europe. I want to show my own culture through song and dance. I want to investigate and research and present my own black history through our own music and words...." Today, the Ailey Company has performed to over 25 million people in the United States, and in 70 countries on six continents, including South Africa. Alvin Ailey's legacy lives on through his muse and former star, Judith Jamison, who, since 1989, continues to foster his vision and broaden his mission even more as artistic director of today's Alvin Ailey American Dance Theatre.

Photograph of Robértu Ras Riley by Edwin Polanco.

SPECIAL THANKS to *Rasta John* and his boys—
Louis, Randy, and El Jay—and don't forget *Pito*.
"I couldn't have done it without you, Ras!"

Stanley Plesent, Esq.

Richard "Dick" Robinson
Scholastic Books, Inc.

Naomi Long Madgett

The poem "Life Dances" *first appeared in* The Crisis, *the magazine-journal of the NAACP, under the title "Aileyesque" in 1977, when Alvin Ailey was awarded the Spingarn Medal, the organization's highest merit of honor.*

Life Dances *may be ordered from bookstores worldwide, including Barnes and Noble, and Amazon.com*

Books may also be ordered at:
www.LifeDancesByRobertu.com